THE
FORAGER'S
PANTRY

Pickled daylily tubers

THE
FORAGER'S
PANTRY

COOKING WITH WILD EDIBLES

ELLEN ZACHOS

PHOTOGRAPHS BY DOUGLAS MERRIAM

GIBBS SMITH
TO ENRICH AND INSPIRE HUMANKIND

First Edition
25 24 23 22 21   5 4 3 2 1

Text © 2021 Ellen Zachos.
Photographs © 2021 Douglas Merriam

Published by
Gibbs Smith
P.O. Box 667
Layton, Utah 84041

1.800.835.4993 orders
www.gibbs-smith.com

Cover and endpapers by Kimberly Glyder
Interior design by Debbie Berne

Printed and bound in China
Gibbs Smith books are printed on either
recycled, 100% post-consumer waste, FSC-
certified papers or on paper produced from
sustainable PEFC-certified forest/controlled
wood source. Learn more at www.pefc.org.

Library of Congress Cataloging-in-
Publication Data

Names: Zachos, Ellen, author. | Merriam,
Douglas, photographer (expression)
Title: The forager's pantry : cooking with
wild edibles / Ellen Zachos ; photographs by
Douglas Merriam.
Description: First edition. | Layton, Utah :
Gibbs Smith, [2021] | Includes index.
Identifiers: LCCN 2020033186 | ISBN
9781423656746 (hardcover) | ISBN
9781423656753 (epub)
Subjects: LCSH: Cooking (Wild foods) |
LCGFT: Cookbooks.
Classification: LCC TX823 .Z33 2021 |
DDC 641.6—dc23
LC record available at https://lccn.loc.
gov/2020033186

I dedicate this book to my mother, Anne Delight Colby Zachos, who died before she could see it in print. Although she was not a forager herself, she loved good food and had a reputation as an excellent cook. She was always eager to try any wild edible I put in front of her.

SPECIAL THANKS

Writing a book during a pandemic has been interesting. It's easy to write and cook when you're socially distanced, but how do you forage for key ingredients that don't grow where you live? Fortunately, foragers are a supportive bunch, and I'm grateful to the many friends who generously sent me ingredients I had intended to gather for myself. Thank you Mark Hardy, Mike Dechter, Kristen Davenport, Erica Marciniac Davis, and Julie Gracie for helping to make this book possible.

I am also grateful to Douglas Merriam who was not only wonderful to work with, but made my food look as good as it tastes. And thanks to Sadie Lowry, a thoughtful, intelligent, and thorough editor.

And as always, thank you to my three favorite proofreaders, Elizabeth Zachos, John Keane, and Michael MacDonald.

Assorted nuts

CONTENTS

....

Lotus roots

INTRODUCTION

. . . .

Do you love to cook? Are you an adventurous eater? Are you a homesteader who wants to be more self-sufficient? Perhaps you're a forager who wants to make the most of your wild harvest, but aren't sure how to get started. Maybe you've been hearing a lot about foraging lately, and you're curious. Not because you want to live off the land or eat wild foods at every meal, but because the flavors sound interesting and you'd like to experiment. But how do you start if you've never cooked with these foods before? If you're reading this book, you've already taken the first step.

I so often hear foragers say they've come home with a huge dock harvest or a gallon of mulberries or bushels of sunchoke tubers, but they don't know what to do with them. You've worked hard to find, harvest, and clean your wild edibles, and it would be a crying shame to let them slowly fade away in the refrigerator while you search for the perfect recipe to highlight their wonderful flavors.

That will never happen to you with the master recipes in this book. This collection of easy, flavorful recipes will be your new best friend in the kitchen, a reference guide that teaches you how to make the most of your wild harvest. We'll start by focusing on flavors of individual ingredients, separated into categories (spices, greens, fruits, etc.). Then we'll explore how to experiment with different techniques, building a set of master recipes from these techniques, so you're comfortable and confident working with your wild harvests.

What is a master recipe? Basically, it's a jumping off point. It gives you a framework for your wild harvests so you can enjoy whatever you bring home. Foraging is unpredictable, and that's part of the adventure. But it can also be a challenge. Let's say you want to make a spring casserole with nettles and garlic mustard, but instead you come home with lamb's quarters and dandelions. *The Forager's Pantry* shows you how to make the appropriate adjustments and substitutions to make a delicious greens casserole with whichever edible greens you harvested.

We'll dive deep into each group of wild foods through flavor profiles, preservation techniques, and master recipes that can be used with a range of ingredients. Additionally, each section will include a few specialty recipes that highlight the unique flavors of specific ingredients.

I've focused on simple recipes, because time is precious. And since foraging takes more time and effort than a quick drive to the grocery store, I bet you'll appreciate some down and dirty advice on how to put together a tasty supper. Besides, when you start with quality ingredients, you don't need to get fancy. The flavors speak for themselves.

The recipes here can almost all be made with materials you already have on hand. You won't have to mail order any unusual ingredients you can't pronounce and will never use again in any other recipe. Combining wild foods with familiar kitchen staples brings new life and excitement to your cooking. My goal is to make this so easy and delicious that you'll want to do it all the time. That's a recipe for success (pun intended).

This book is a kitchen guide, not a field guide. If you need help with plant identification, I have loads of excellent recommendations in the reference section at the back of this book, and I suggest you use them in conjunction with this book for a safe and satisfying wild foods experience. Remember, the number one rule of foraging is that if you're not 100% sure about what you're harvesting, *don't harvest it*! You should never put anything in your mouth that you can't identify with absolute certainty. Period. No exceptions.

Foraging is only fun when it's safe, so here are a few more guidelines. It's important to forage in clean places where your harvest will be free of pollutants. A golf course or botanical garden with a perfectly manicured landscape is not someplace I'd recommend foraging—the chemicals used to maintain that perfection are not chemicals you want to ingest. If you forage in city parks, keep an eye open for signs indicating that the area has been sprayed with pesticides or herbicides. Most parks post signs when they do this kind of work.

Foraged food is organic. Most of the time. No one sprays pokeweed with insecticides to keep the insects at bay, but that doesn't mean all wild foods are untainted. A safe forager is an observant forager, and you need to be on the lookout for signs of herbicides wherever you forage. I've seen park rangers spray the delicious native cow parsnip because they thought it was giant hogweed (which can cause serious contact rashes). I wish our park system had the time and money to better educate our rangers, but it doesn't. So it's up to you to look for signs of chemical damage like unusually curled or deformed foliage or swaths of dead plants. Remember, many wild edibles are considered weeds by people who practice commercial agriculture, and it's not unusual for them to try to eliminate these weeds from their cultivated fields.

Foraging by the side of the road is often tempting due to easy access, but it's not always a good idea. Vehicle exhaust may contain heavy metals (like lead, nickel, cadmium, etc.) that settle out of the exhaust and are absorbed by plant roots. Leaves and stems will contain more of these than fruits and nuts. Plants growing uphill from a busy highway will be safer than plants growing downhill, because the heavy metal particulates are washed downhill by rain. Personally, I wouldn't harvest within 50 feet downhill from an interstate, but on the uphill side, I might feel safe at 30 to 40 feet. Foraging next to a country road where traffic is light is a much safer prospect.

Ask permission! If you pass a house with a giant black walnut tree out front and loads of nuts on the ground, knock on the door and ask if you can collect them. Most likely the homeowner will thank you for cleaning up the lawn, and on the off chance that the answer is no, at least you've done the honorable thing.

In public places, check the rules before you harvest. Most state and national parks have established rules about foraging that you can look up with a simple web search. Look for "park name" + "Superintendent's Compendium," then read through the document to see what's allowed and what isn't. Many parks allow limited foraging for fruits and nuts, with quantities varying from park to park. And just to be on the safe side, print up a copy of the relevant rules to keep in your pocket while you're out there. You might be surprised at how many park rangers don't know the rules about foraging.

Do you have food allergies? If so, you'll need to do a little research. For example, if you're allergic to aspirin, you might want to stay away from wintergreen (*Gaultheria procumbens*), which is a natural source of salicylic acid, an ingredient in aspirin. If you react badly to mangoes or cashews, you might stay away from sumac, which is in the same plant family: *Anacardiaceae*. Your decision will depend on how allergic you are and how willing you are to take a risk. Make sure your choice is an educated one by learning which plants and mushrooms are related to your known food allergens.

Depending on where you forage, you might want to go with a friend. I know some people don't want to share their special spots, but personally, I enjoy foraging with a friend much more than going alone. Not only because there's safety in numbers, although it's true that both bears and humans are less likely to mess with a group than a single hiker; I like foraging with friends because the joy of discovery is something that increases when it is shared.

Sustainability. It's a buzz word these days, and one that's of the utmost importance for foragers. It can be hard to harvest in moderation when you find something unusual and delicious. You get excited! You want it all! But remember, you're not the only one out there in search of food. It's important to leave a good portion behind to feed animals and insects, not to mention other foragers. It's also important to leave some of the plant behind so it can propagate itself. If you're harvesting fern fiddleheads, for example, never take more than a few from each plant, leaving more than you harvest so the plant can continue to photosynthesize. If you take all of the foliage, that plant won't come back next year.

If a tasty plant is endangered in your area, explore alternatives. For example, ramps are a much sought-after wild member of the onion family, but in some parts of the country, they're overharvested. As slow growers, ramps may take years to recover from being over picked. Field garlic, a closely related cousin, is generally considered an obnoxious weed wherever it pops up. It has excellent flavor, is easy to harvest, and grows abundantly—you won't make a dent in the population. So why not focus on the field garlic and leave the ramps alone? Or, if you must have ramps, harvest no more than a single leaf from each plant. Leave a leaf behind to photosynthesize, and leave the bulb in the ground to store energy for next year's growth.

Foraging is seasonal. There's lots of talk about local, seasonal food these days and with good reason. Food picked at the peak of ripeness is at its most delicious. No one harvests black raspberries when they're still green to make them easier to ship. We foragers get them when they're at their best: sweet, juicy, soft, and with a very short shelf life. The only way to experience this warm, wonderful summer fruit is to get out there in season and pick it yourself.

Speaking of seasonality, the harvest season for every wild food varies depending on your location. Cattail flowers might be a summer crop in New Hampshire and a spring harvest in North Carolina. It's more important to consider your climate than your calendar when you're wondering what's in season.

Most of the plants and mushrooms in this book can be found across a wide range of locations. I've chosen them to make the book as useful as possible to as many people as possible. The resources in the back of the book will help you explore further when you're ready.

End of lecture! We're ready to dive into the fun stuff: the recipes. There's more info on equipment and plant education at the back of the book, but right now, it's time to roll up our sleeves and head into the kitchen.

Spruce tips

SPICES
AND HERBS

· ·

Using spices and herbs is one of the easiest ways to
jazz up your cooking, and wild spices and herbs are
amazingly flavorful. Some are similar to familiar
spices, and some of them will rock your world with
their unique flavors. In every case, playing with wild
herbs and spices is a great introduction to wild foods.

What's the difference between an herb and a spice? In general, herbs are the leaves, flowers, and stems of herbaceous plants. They are delicate plant tissues. Spices are the barks, roots, and seeds, i.e. the woodier plant parts. Whether a wild edible is a spice or an herb will determine how you preserve it and how you cook with it. Sturdy spices stand up better to long cooking times than more delicate herbs.

Fresh or dry? There's no reason why you can't use both. Most foragers use fresh ingredients immediately after harvesting, and then dry the remainder to use throughout the year. Drying intensifies the flavor of both herbs and spices because it removes the water and leaves behind the essential oils, phenolic acids, flavonoids, etc. If you're following a recipe that calls for fresh herbs and all you have is dried, you'll need to adjust the amount you use. A general rule is to use two to four times as much fresh as you would dried. If a recipe requires a long cooking time, you'll probably want to use dried herbs and spices. The more robust the flavor of the herb or spice, the longer it maintains its taste when cooked.

Will you preserve your harvest whole or ground? It's convenient to have ground spices on hand, ready to use, but grinding speeds up oxidation and the deterioration of flavor. I recommend keeping your herbs and spices whole and grinding them just before you use them. Usually I prefer an electric spice grinder[1], which creates a very fine powder. A mortar and pestle is useful for a coarser grind.

Herbs and spices can be sweet or savory. They can also be warm, sharp, hot, or bitter, or they may deliver that hard-to-define umami goodness everyone loves. Think about the herbs and spices you use most often in your cooking and why you like them. That will help you figure out which wild flavors you want to experiment with first.

A few of the plants I recommend in this chapter come with warnings. I realize this may make people nervous, so I want to be totally transparent. The fact is that some of the traditional spices we eat every day contain compounds that would be dangerous *if* they were eaten in large quantities. For example, both nutmeg and cinnamon contain multiple chemicals that should only be consumed in small amounts. As long as we use them as spices, not foods, we're safe.

---

1. I keep a separate coffee bean grinder just for spices. I love the flavor of coffee, but don't want it mixed with my wild herbs and spices.

The same goes for several of the foraged herbs and spices in this chapter: sassafras roots and twigs, sweet clover, and wild ginger rhizomes. The key is in the dosage. Use these plants as herbs and spices, rather than food, and you should be safe (unless you have a specific allergy to the plant).

Preserving the Harvest

Foraging is a seasonal business, so preserving the harvest is necessary if you want to enjoy these unbuyable flavors year-round. Herbs and spices are easy to preserve, and you have your choice of two methods: dehydration and freezing.

DEHYDRATION

If you don't have a dehydrator yet, put it on your wish list! Mine has paid for itself many times over. It's especially important to me that it has a timer and that the temperature is adjustable, two features that frequently don't come with lower-priced models.

If you live someplace humid, a dehydrator is essential for drying herbs, spices, fruit leather, fruit, and mushrooms. Even in dry climates, a dehydrator is useful because of its stacked shelves and compact size. Herbs and spices are best dried at 95°F or lower—their volatile oils, which are preserved at lower temperatures, are where the flavor is. Dehydrators usually get the job done in less than a day, depending on the humidity where you live and what you're drying.

Of course, you can dry food without a dehydrator. If you do this outside, a double-screen setup works best. The mesh allows air to circulate from above and below and protects your harvest from pilfering birds and mammals. Several companies make net-covered collapsible shelves you can hang in a breezy spot. Drying your harvest this way may take several days.

You may also bundle and hang your harvest in a dry, dark place inside your home. This method may take several weeks. Once everything is dry, transfer your herbs and spices to a sealed glass jar and store that in a dark place to preserve color and flavor. Don't be fooled by those pretty magazine photos of country kitchens all decked out with photogenic bunches of dried herbs. Those herbs are either staged for the photo, considered purely decorative, or have just finished drying and are about to be transferred into glass jars for long-term storage.

Oven drying is ok, but only ok. Most ovens can't be set below 170°F, which means you'll lose flavor as the oils volatilize. If that's all you've got, that's what you'll use. Crack open the door of your oven to lower the internal oven temperature.

It's also possible to dry herbs in a microwave. Microwaves work by exposing food to electromagnetic radiation, which in turn creates heat. To dry them this way, lay your herbs in a single layer on a dry paper towel and microwave at full power for 30-second intervals until the herbs are crisp. If the paper towel becomes wet, replace it. As with oven drying, you'll lose some flavor this way due to the high temperatures created by the microwave. But at least you won't be heating your kitchen with an open oven. Be sure to let your herbs cool before you transfer them to a jar. Otherwise, condensation may form during cooldown, which will partially rehydrate your herbs and could lead to mold.

Dried herbs don't take up freezer space, don't require canning, and last for several years. If you can't identify the dried herb by smelling it, it's too old to have any flavor and you should throw it away. Not because it will hurt you, but because the whole point of this is flavor, right?

FREEZING

Some herbs and spices can be preserved by freezing, which maintains volatile oils and therefore conserves flavor. There are several freezing techniques to explore.

Fresh herbs can be chopped and frozen with oil in ice cube trays to preserve their flavor and color. This works especially well for things which may be later cooked with oil, like wild garlic and bee balm. You can adjust this technique and fill those ice cube trays with broth or water if that aligns with how you'll eventually use the herb. Once your cubes have frozen, transfer them to a sealed container or vacuum seal them and keep them in the freezer. They'll last for at least a year this way.

Blanching your herbs before freezing helps preserve their vibrant colors and flavors by impeding enzyme activity that leads to decomposition. Bring a pot of water to a boil and use tongs to swish your herbs around until the leaves turn bright green, which should take 10–15 seconds. Immediately move the herbs to a bowl of ice water to stop the cooking (this is called shocking the herbs).

Dried bee balm flowers and leaves can be easily substituted for oregano.

Spicebush berries are best preserved by a combination of drying and freezing. This fruit contains lots of fats that make them an excellent energy source for wildlife. It also means the fruit spoils quickly and may become rancid, even after drying. I dry my spicebush berries, freeze them whole, and grind them immediately before using. You may also freeze fresh spicebush berries, but they'll be too soft to grind into a powder once they've thawed. You'd have to use them whole, to infuse cream or alcohol, or as a paste.

Seasonal Availability

Like most wild edibles, herbs and spices are seasonal. Your exact harvest time will depend on your location, but here's a table to get you started.

	Spring	Summer	Fall	Winter
bee balm (*Monarda* spp.)	X	X	X	
cow parsnip seed (*Heracleum maximum*)		X	X	
field garlic (*Allium vineale*)	X		X	
juniper berries (*Juniperus* spp.)	X	X	X	X
mugwort (*Artemisia vulgaris*)	X	X		
mushroom powder (various species)	X	X	X	X
pink peppercorns (*Schinus molle*)			X	X
prickly ash (*Zanthoxylum americanum*)			X	
sassafras (*Sassafras albidum*)	X	X	X	X
spicebush berries (*Lindera benzoin*)			X	
spruce tips (*Picea* spp.)	X	X		
sumac (*Rhus* spp.)		X	X	
sweet clover (*Melilotus* spp.)		X	X	
wild ginger (*Asarum* spp.)	X		X	X
wintergreen (*Gaultheria procumbens*)	X	X	X	X

Bee balm (*Monarda* spp.) is a popular garden plant and a very tasty herb. The taste varies from species to species, but in general, it's very similar to oregano, sometimes with a lemony edge. Both the flowers and leaves can be used fresh and dry.

Poor, misunderstood cow parsnip (*Heracleum maximum*). All too often, this tasty native plant is misidentified as giant hogweed, a plant that causes painful skin rashes. I've seen cow parsnip drenched with herbicides in a misguided attempt to protect hikers and it makes me want to weep. Despite being one of my favorite spices, cow parsnip seed has a flavor I find difficult to describe. It's herbal, citrusy, slightly bitter, perhaps reminiscent of celery? Give it a taste; you won't be sorry! Persian cuisine uses a cow parsnip cousin in bean and lentil dishes: *H. persicum* (aka golpar or Persian hogweed). You may harvest seeds when they're green or brown; the flavor will be slightly different depending on which you harvest. Either way, dry your cow parsnip seeds for long-term storage.

Field garlic (*Allium vineale*), or wild garlic, is a weed that lawn lovers despise. It looks like grass in sunny fields and yards, but is slightly darker green. It also grows faster than grass; several days after mowing, field garlic gives an uneven texture to the lawn. Small bulbs (¼–½ inch in diameter) grow in clumps—though the bulbs often grow singly in shadier spots—and the stems can grow to 24 inches tall. Harvest the bulbs in spring or fall when they're full of flavor—when the plant is in active growth in summer, the bulbs will be more fibrous and less tasty. The flavor of field garlic resembles a combination of onion and garlic. Preserve field garlic bulbs by drying or by blanching, chopping, then freezing in cubes.

Juniper berries (*Juniperus* spp.) are best known for the flavor they add to gin and sauerkraut, but they can be used for much more than that. The fruit should be harvested when it's blue or purple—green fruit is unripe and intensely bitter. *J. virginiana* and *J. communis*, the two most common species in the United States, both produce tasty fruit. A European juniper species (*J. sabina*) is believed to be toxic to cattle that graze on its foliage, bark, and berries, but no human studies have been conducted. Dry juniper berries for long-term storage.

Mugwort (*Artemisia vulgaris*) is an underappreciated plant. While most Americans consider it a weed, other cultures value mugwort as an herb. In Asia, you'll find mugwort noodles and rice cakes. Used with goose and duck in Germany, mugwort is known as "the mother of herbs" because it's considered so versatile. With its aggressive growth habit, mugwort would be difficult to overharvest. The flavor may remind you of sage, but it's even more interesting. Use mugwort fresh or dried.

Mushroom powder delivers an umami flavor. You can mix it with salt or, if you're on a reduced-sodium diet, use it in place of salt altogether. Sprinkle it directly on eggs, soups, or popcorn, or bake it into sauces and casseroles. Some mushrooms make more flavorful powder than others, like black-staining polypore, porcini, and hen of the woods. Dry your mushrooms and grind them just before using to maintain optimum flavor.

Pink peppercorns (*Schinus molle, S. terebinthifolia*) are often found in pepper blends, although they are not true peppercorns. These are warm climate trees. In the United States, you'll find them growing in Florida, Texas, Puerto Rico, Hawaii, and in California as far north as the Bay Area. Like sumac, pink peppercorns are members of the family *Anacardiaceae*, which also includes cashews and mangoes. If you're allergic to either of those, you might also be allergic to pink peppercorns, so make an informed decision. *S. terebinthifolia* is generally considered invasive, while *S. molle* has a less aggressive growth habit (although it's considered invasive in CA). This spice is best preserved by drying.

Prickly ash (*Zanthoxylum americanum*) is related to Szechuan pepper, sharing many of the same flavor characteristics: citrusy, peppery, warm, and somewhat numbing. It's the rind of the prickly ash fruit that has the flavor. Discard the fruit inside; it's gritty and flavorless. Use ground prickly ash in dry rubs, marinades, and sauces. Toasting the spice or infusing it in olive oil intensifies the flavor. Drying is the best way to preserve prickly ash.

Sassafras (*Sassafras albidum*) has fascinated me since I was a child—I loved that a single tree could produce three different leaf shapes. As a forager, I'm impressed that this single plant produces an herb and two spices. The dried leaves of the sassafras tree add a lemon flavor to soups and stews and act as a thickener. Sassafras twigs can be decocted[2] to make a lemony syrup, and the roots and root bark of sassafras trees are one of the original spices used to flavor root beer. Drying is the best way to preserve all parts of the sassafras tree.

Spicebush berries (*Lindera benzoin*) are strongly flavored, warm, and spicy. This may be my favorite wild spice, although I'd rather not be forced to choose. (I get very nervous when my stash is low.) I use it in place of cinnamon and

---

2. To decoct something is to make a strong tea by boiling the ingredients. This is different from an infusion, which is made by pouring just-boiled water onto the ingredients.

nutmeg. Its flavor resembles allspice but with a little more sweetness and a peppery edge. It's wonderful in both sweet and savory dishes—once you taste it, you won't want to be without it. Spicebush berries can be used fresh or dried.

Spruce tips (*Picea* spp.) can be harvested as long as they are soft and pale green. It's easy to tell the difference between young tips and older growth just by touching them or looking at the tip of the branch. Spruce tips contain lots of vitamin C and were historically used to prevent scurvy back when that was a thing. The flavor is citrusy and reminiscent of rosemary. Spruce tips have the best flavor fresh or frozen.

Sumac (*Rhus* spp.) berries are a tart delight, often used in Mediterranean and Middle Eastern spice mixes. In the United States, people fear mistaking edible sumac for poison sumac. Let me put your mind at ease: the fruit of edible sumac is red and the fruit of poison sumac is white. Since you only harvest when the fruit is ripe, if you can tell the difference between red and white, you'll be ok. If you're color-blind (and I'm not joking), take someone with you when you forage. Sumac fruit makes a lemony beverage and is best used dried.

Sweet clover (*Melilotus* spp.), or melilot, is a weed that grows from coast to coast. Yellow-flowered (*M. officinalis*) and white-flowered (*M. albus*) sweet clover taste exactly the same to me. The flavor is reminiscent of vanilla, and both the flowers and leaves can be used in place of tarragon. This is a plant that must be thoroughly dried to be safe. If the plant gets moldy, throw it out. Like several other spices (e.g. cinnamon, nutmeg), sweet clover contains coumarin, which is an anticoagulant. Fungus may interact with the naturally occurring coumarin to create dicoumarol, which, when consumed in large quantities, can prevent blood clotting and cause hemorrhaging. The amounts recommended in this book are perfectly safe. Sweet clover may be used fresh or dry (just not halfway in between).

Wild ginger (*Asarum canadense, A. caudatum*) shares the spice and warmth of its tropical grocery store cousin, but with more darkness and complexity. The underground rhizomes can be harvested without damaging the plant. Dig up a clump, snip the rhizome connecting the plants, then replant the (now) two plants. Some people worry that eating wild ginger puts them at risk for aristolochic acid poisoning. I've read the science and do not consider this a risk.[3] If

---

3. Again, it's a question of dosage. Wild ginger does contain some aristolochic acid, but the recorded poisonings are related to different plants consumed in greater quantity and different forms than what is recommended here.

you're worried, I suggest you do some research, too, and make a decision you're comfortable with. Wild ginger is delicious fresh or dried.

Wintergreen (*Gaultheria procumbens*) is a tiny evergreen shrub that acts as a groundcover in acidic soils with a low pH of between 4.5 and 5.5. Its pretty red berries add color to infusions but have a mealy texture. The most flavor comes from barely fermenting the leaves in room-temperature water or infusing them in alcohol. Wintergreen can be harvested year-round, but it's easiest to spot in winter when the surrounding herbaceous plants have died back to the ground. Fresh wintergreen is best, and it is available twelve months a year.

EASY SUBSTITUTIONS

Substituting wild herbs and spices for familiar herbs and spices is one of the easiest ways to get started with wild flavors. Here are some simple suggestions.

Substitute this	for this!
field garlic	commercial garlic
spruce tips	rosemary
mugwort	sage
bee balm	oregano
sumac	lemon
sweet clover	tarragon, vanilla
spicebush berries	cinnamon, nutmeg, allspice
prickly ash	Szechuan pepper
pink peppercorns	black pepper
wild ginger	tropical ginger
mushroom powder	MSG

General Techniques

You've harvested your herbs and spices, and maybe even preserved some for future use. Now you're ready to use them. Here are a few general techniques you can use to turn those herbs and spices into useful kitchen flavorings.

SUGARS

Sugars work best with dried herbs. To create an herbal or spiced sugar, pulverize your herb or spice in a grinder with an equal amount of sugar. This flavored sugar can be used in cookies, cakes, or the toppings of fruit crisps and crumbles. Try it with spicebush berries, sumac, pink peppercorns, sweet clover, or spruce tips.

SALT

For savory applications, you can repeat the above process with salt instead of sugar. This should only be done with dried herbs and spices so you can keep the flavored salt on your counter without refrigeration. Dried mushrooms, juniper berries, field garlic, bee balm, sumac, cow parsnip seed, prickly ash, and pink peppercorns all make excellent flavored salts. Spruce tip salt is also delicious, but it should be kept refrigerated if made with fresh or frozen spruce tips.

COMPOUND BUTTERS

Fresh herbs make delicious compound butters, which can be used immediately or frozen for storage. Soften a stick of butter by leaving it at room temperature in a small bowl. Mince two to three tablespoons of your foraged herb (less for strongly flavored herbs, more for subtle herbs), and add that to the bowl. Mash it all together, then transfer the butter to a piece of parchment paper. Shape the butter into a roll, wrap it in the paper, and refrigerate.

When the butter has hardened, slice off pieces as needed. You might also freeze a big chunk for up to six months, but be sure to store the wrapped butter in a freezer bag to preserve its flavor. You can use this on bread, rice, pasta, popcorn, or in sauces for meat and fish.

CREAM

An herbal or spiced cream infusion can be used in all sorts of things. Savory infusions can be added to mashed potatoes, casseroles, or sauces, and sweet infusions make flavorful puddings, panna cottas, and ice creams. The amount of herb or spice will depend on how strong its flavor is and how well that flavor infuses in fat. (Cream is deliciously fatty.) When making a cream infusion, you'll heat—but not boil—the cream, then cover, allowing the liquid to cool and infuse, and then strain off the solids.

VINEGAR

There's almost nothing easier than infusing vinegar with herbs and spices, and some foraged ingredients add color as well as flavor, such as red bee balm flowers, sumac berries, and pink peppercorns. I like to use rice wine vinegar because of its mild flavor, but you could certainly infuse other kinds of vinegar as well. In a pint jar with a tight-fitting lid, combine three tablespoons of dried herb with one pint of vinegar. Cover the jar, let it sit for three weeks, then strain off the solids and transfer the flavored vinegar to a clean container. Use this as a base for a vinaigrette or in a flavorful marinade.

ALCOHOL

Some herbs and spices make excellent alcohol extracts, which can be used as flavorings in baking. Infusing wintergreen leaves and berries in vodka creates a flavorful extract to use in ice cream, frosting, cakes, and cookies. You can also infuse other spirits with herbs or spices to make unique wildcrafted cocktails. Think spicebush berries in rum, sumac fruit in gin, and pink peppercorns in tequila.

CALCULATING VOLUME

It's not always easy to anticipate how the volume of whole herbs and spices will translate into powdered herbs and spices. A good general rule is to start with ⅓ more of the whole herb than you want to end up with in powdered form. For example, 1½ teaspoons of dried field garlic bulbs will give you about 1 teaspoon of field garlic powder.

DRY RUB

I love having a really solid dry rub on hand, especially if I'm not feeling creative around supper time. A foraged dry rub makes the ordinary extraordinary. Use it to coat chicken thighs, pork chops, salmon fillets . . . pretty much anything.

Salt and a little sugar are excellent additions to a dry rub. The sugar helps with caramelization if you're searing meat, and salt just always helps everything.

This is a recipe you can play around with, mixing and matching the herbs and spices to create your perfect blend. Remember that some flavors are stronger than others and that certain herbs and spices combine better with certain dishes. Consider starting with no more than four different flavors so you can appreciate each one of them. And there's no reason why you can't create multiple blends for different dishes.

Substituting is easy. If you don't have field garlic, try dried ramps or nodding onion. Ground sumac, sassafras, or spruce tips all have a citrusy flavor and could substitute for bee balm. Wild ginger is spicy and warm; if you don't have any, try cow parsnip seed or juniper berries. (Juniper berries are very strong, so reduce the quantity by half.) Sweet clover might take the place of spicebush berries.

YIELD: 4 GENEROUS TEASPOONS

1 teaspoon dried, powdered field garlic bulbs

1/4 teaspoon dried, powdered bee balm leaves or flowers

1/2 teaspoon dried, powdered wild ginger rhizomes

1/2 teaspoon dried, powdered spicebush berries

1 teaspoon brown sugar

1 teaspoon salt

Grind each of the 4 spices individually, then combine in a small bowl and add the sugar and salt. Taste and adjust as needed.

You can store dry rub in a spice jar or plastic container with a tight-fitting lid, but since the spices have been ground, use them as quickly as possible before the flavor deteriorates.

NOTE: Mugwort doesn't grind into a powder, making it challenging to use in a dry rub. The flavor is wonderful, and it's a great herb, but it comes out looking and feeling more like dryer lint, so don't freak out when you see what it looks like after grinding.

VINAIGRETTE

It's easy to keep a jar of this vinaigrette on hand, and foraged ingredients make a fresher, healthier salad dressing than commercial salad dressings, which may contain polyunsaturated oils, artificial flavorings, and preservatives.

YIELD: A SCANT $1/2$ CUP

3 tablespoons infused vinegar (see page 26)

1 teaspoon Dijon mustard

$1/4$ cup olive oil

$1/2$ teaspoon ground pink peppercorns

1 teaspoon honey

Combine all of the ingredients in a pint jar and shake it like crazy. Or whisk the ingredients together in a bowl and transfer to a jar for storage.

You could substitute cow parsnip seed for the sweet clover, ramps for the field garlic, or maple syrup for the honey. Add a little ground sumac or sassafras for some lemony flavor or prickly ash for its indefinable citrusy, woodsy quality.

NOTE: If you decide to use prickly ash, try dry roasting it for 30–60 seconds before grinding to improve the flavor and lessen the numbing quality. Or grind it first, then warm the powder in the olive oil, and use that oil in your salad dressing.

SPICE SYRUPS

These syrups are very versatile. Combine them with seltzer for a homemade soda, with booze for a unique cocktail, with vinegar or mustard (or both!) for a flavorful marinade, with cream for ice cream, or with fruit for a sorbet. Syrups don't have to be overwhelmingly sweet. Sure, they're made with sugar, but when the herb or spice you choose is savory or spicy, the end result can be surprising and delicious.

The amount of spice or herb you use will depend on whether it is fresh or dry and how strong the flavor of the herb or spice is. In general, I suggest using equal parts fresh herb/spice + sugar + water. If you're using dried herbs and spices, use $1/2$ part herb/ spice + 1 part water + 1 part sugar. However, for juniper berries and pink peppercorns, $1/2$ part fresh spice (or $1/4$ part dried spice) will give you a very flavorful result.

I use white sugar for most syrups because it has the most neutral flavor of any sweetener I know. Feel free to use your favorite sweetener, but be aware that some bring their own flavor to the party.

You'll start by making a very strong tea. Because this tea will be diluted when you combine the syrup with other ingredients, it needs to be stronger than a tea made to drink as is. The process is slightly different for herbs and spices because of the different densities of the plant materials. Herbs can be infused in just-boiled water, while spices require actual boiling (aka decocting).

1 part fresh herbs/spices or $1/2$ part dried herbs/spices

1 part water

Sugar (the amount will vary)

For an herbal syrup, pour just-boiled water over your herb, cover, and let it sit for an hour. For a spiced syrup, combine the spice and water in a sauce pan and bring the mixture to a boil. Reduce the heat to a simmer, cover, and let it cook for 30 minutes.

Strain off the solids, measure the liquid, return it to the pan, and add an equal volume of sugar. You'll lose some liquid to absorption and evaporation during infusion and decoction. Therefore, you'll need less than a full "part" of sugar to make your syrups. Warm the syrup, whisking to dissolve the sugar. Rub a bit of the syrup between two fingers and when you can no longer feel the grains of the sugar, it's done.

Transfer your syrup to a container with a tight-fitting lid. This will keep in the refrigerator for several weeks, or may be canned in a boiling water bath for longer storage.

CHAI MASALA

I had to look up the difference between *chai masala* and *masala chai*. *Chai masala* refers to the spiced tea blend, and *masala chai* is the tea made from that blend. In India, the spices used to compose a *chai masala* traditionally include cardamom, cinnamon, cloves, and ginger with black tea and milk. But since *masala* basically means spice blend, there's no reason why you can't create your own.

YIELD: 1 CUP

1 teaspoon dried wild ginger rhizomes

$\frac{1}{8}$ teaspoon dried sweet clover

$\frac{1}{4}$ teaspoon dried spicebush berries

$\frac{1}{2}$ teaspoon dried cow parsnip seeds

$\frac{1}{4}$ teaspoon spruce tips (fresh or frozen)

2 dried juniper berries

1 cup water

1 tablespoon loose black tea leaves or 1 tea bag unflavored black tea

$\frac{1}{2}$ cup milk

Honey, to taste

Combine the spices and water in a saucepan and bring the water to a boil. Reduce the heat, cover the pan, and simmer for 15 minutes.

Remove the pan from the heat and add the tea. If you're using a tea bag, cut it open and pour the tea leaves directly into the hot water. Stir to combine, cover, and let the mixture steep for 2 minutes.

Add the milk and honey. (I like a teaspoon; my husband prefers no sweetener. To each their own.) Return the mixture to the heat and bring it back to a boil. Remove from the heat and strain the liquid into a mug.

The above makes 1 cup of wild *masala chai*. You can premix the herbs and spices and keep the mix on hand in a sealed jar so you won't have to do the mixing each time you want a cup. This blend also makes a lovely spicy tea jelly or tea cocktail.

NOTE: I don't think garlic would work well in this recipe, but every other spice in this chapter does, even the pink peppercorns. If you have a favorite, start with that, then play with the combinations until you find your personal favorite.

PANNA COTTA

This recipe works with any number of spices, but I most love to serve it with spruce tips because nobody expects a green dessert. If you don't have spruce nearby, this can also be made with fir tips or the tips of young, evergreen hemlock branches. (Those would be from the evergreen hemlock tree, *not* the herbaceous poison hemlock plant!)

YIELD: 6 (4-OUNCE) SERVINGS

1 cup evergreen tips

2 cups heavy cream

1 cup whole milk

$^1/_2$ tablespoon unflavored gelatin powder

1 tablespoon cold water

$2^1/_2$ tablespoons sugar

Combine the spruce tips, milk, and cream in a blender, using a low to medium speed to break up the needles. You don't need to pulverize the spruce tips, but breaking up the needles increases their surface area and releases more flavor. I don't use the high setting on my Vitamix because I'm afraid that might churn the cream into butter.

Refrigerate the infused cream/milk overnight or for up to 24 hours.

herb/spice quantity adjustments	
ground ginger rhizomes	1 tablespoon
ground spicebush berries	3 tablespoons
ground sweet clover	2 tablespoons
sassafras root bark	2 tablespoons
sumac powder	4 tablespoons
wintergreen extract	1 tablespoon

Strain the liquid, pressing on the needles to remove as much liquid as possible. You'll probably want to do a second straining or squeeze the cream through a jelly bag or cheesecloth to catch the little bits of solid matter. You should end up with about 3 cups of dairy.

Sprinkle the gelatin on top of the water to let the gelatin bloom. It will be ready by the time you need it.

Combine the cream/milk and sugar in a saucepan and bring it just to a simmer, then remove the pan from the heat. Whisk in the bloomed gelatin until it's completely dissolved. Rub a little of the liquid between your fingers to make sure it's silky, not grainy. If it's grainy, keep whisking until the liquid is smooth.

continued

As soon as the gelatin has fully dissolved, place the saucepan in an ice bath (a shallow pot filled halfway with a combination of ice cubes and water). Sit the bottom of the saucepan in the ice and whisk the cream until it's lukewarm. You'll know you've reached this point when the liquid feels neither warm nor cold against your finger. This is an essential step. Without it, the texture of your panna cotta will not be right.

Pour the lukewarm liquid into mini-canning jars or ramekins and refrigerate until jiggly (4 hours or overnight). I use 4-ounce canning jars because each one has its own lid, which is convenient. Plus they're cute. Dessert should appeal to both the eyes and the stomach, don't you think?

Your spruce tip panna cotta can be served plain, but if you happen to have some spruce tip syrup in the back of your refrigerator, pour a drizzle onto each serving for an extra shot of flavor.

All panna cotta made with ground or powdered spices should be strained a second time through a yogurt strainer or jelly bag to remove as many solids as possible.

BLOOMING GELATIN

Blooming gelatin is an important step in making many delicious desserts. It's what gives panna cotta its wiggle and Jell-O its jiggle. Sprinkle the gelatin onto cold water and let it sit for five minutes. The gelatin has fully bloomed when the surface of the liquid has a wrinkled skin, with very few gelatin grains visible. This should take no more than five minutes. The cold liquid may be water, juice, or dairy, depending on the recipe. At this point, the bloomed gelatin is ready to be added to warmed liquid. Blooming gelatin in warm liquid does not thoroughly allow all the gelatin grains to soften and you may end up with lumps or strings of a gelatinous mess.

HERB & CHEESE
QUICK BREAD

Sometimes I don't have the patience to make a bread that needs to sit and rise, in which case I make this quick bread. The texture and flavor are superb, the recipe is easy, and you can use any number of wild herbs and cheeses to keep the flavor combinations interesting. I first made it with bee balm and feta, but I've loved every combo I've tried.

YIELD: 1 (9 X 5-INCH) LOAF

1¼ cups all-purpose flour

1 tablespoon baking powder

⅓ teaspoon salt

½ teaspoon pepper

3 tablespoons dried, crumbled bee balm

3 large eggs

¼ cup olive oil

½ cup Greek yogurt

2 cups grated cheese of choice

Preheat the oven to 350°F and spray a 9 x 5-inch loaf pan with nonstick cooking spray.

In a large bowl, combine the flour, baking powder, salt, pepper, and foraged herbs.

In another bowl, whisk together the eggs, olive oil, and yogurt. Fold the wet ingredients into the dry ingredients, then gently incorporate the cheese. I like feta, mozzarella, or a sharp cheddar.

herb/spice quantity adjustments	
field garlic powder	3 tablespoons
cow parsnip seed	2 tablespoons
mugwort	6 tablespoons
mushroom powder	6 tablespoons
pink peppercorns	1 tablespoon
sumac powder	4½ tablespoons

Transfer the batter to the loaf pan and bake for 30 minutes or until a skewer inserted in the center comes out clean. Let the bread cool in the pan for 10 minutes, then turn it out and let it cool completely. Serve with a skim of butter.

NOTES: If you make this recipe with pink peppercorns, leave out the black pepper.

If you make this with mugwort, remember that mugwort has a very interesting texture when ground. Unlike many spices, it doesn't form a pourable powder. Instead it becomes fluffy. Don't freak out, it's normal.

Transfer the ground mugwort to a bowl and add enough water to hydrate the herb. You'll have to stir it together because the mugwort is so light that it floats on the water. Once it's been hydrated, pour the herb into a strainer to drain. Press the liquid out of the mugwort, then use as directed above.

JAPANESE STEAMED BUNS

I first made these buns with mugwort, an herb that is often used in Asian cooking. The green color and herbal flavor are lovely. This recipe also works well with sumac, sweet clover, cow parsnip seeds, or spicebush berries. The buns are light and airy, a little sweet, a little savory. They make a great side dish or a nice snack with a cup of tea.

Because these buns are steamed, you'll need a sauté pan large enough to hold a 6-muffin tin.

YIELD: 6 BUNS

3 tablespoons ground mugwort

1 egg, beaten

1 tablespoon vegetable oil

3 tablespoons milk

3 tablespoons sugar

$3/4$ cup Bisquick (or similar pancake mix)

Grind enough dried mugwort leaves to make 3 tablespoons of ground herb. Remember mugwort's unusual texture? Hydrate the ground mugwort by stirring it with water to combine, then pour it through a strainer to drain.

herb/spice quantity adjustments	
sumac powder	2 tablespoons
ground ginger	2 tablespoons
spicebush berries	2 tablespoons
pink peppercorns	2 tablespoons

While the mugwort is draining, combine the egg, vegetable oil, milk, and sugar in a bowl. Add the Bisquick and drained mugwort and stir to combine. The batter will be thin (like pancakes!) and green.

Grease the muffin tin or line with cupcake liners, then distribute the batter evenly among the 6 cups. Place the cupcake tin in a large sauté pan, and add about a half inch of water to the pan. Cover, and turn the heat on medium high.

Steam the buns for 12–15 minutes until they are round and puffy. Check at about 10 minutes to make sure the water hasn't all boiled off, and if it has, add more to the sauté pan. The buns are ready to eat when you can feel them bounce back from (but not stick to) the gentle push of a fingertip.

These mugwort steamed buns are best served warm. Leftovers can be reheated in a steamer or microwave.

NOTES: If you make these with any herb other than mugwort, you can skip the hydration step and add the ground herb or spice directly to the other ingredients.

I have made these with several wild spices that were not successful, so why not learn from my mistakes? Steamed buns with cow parsnip seed were bitter, sassafras leaf powder contributed no discernible flavor, and sweet clover was merely meh.

HERB/SPICE MAYO

Have you ever made your own mayonnaise? It's not difficult at all, and making your own allows you to use any wild flavoring you'd like. This recipe works well with field garlic, bee balm, sumac, cow parsnip seed, mushroom powder, juniper berries, and pink peppercorns. You'll need a hand blender or small food processor for this (yes, you *could* do it by hand with a whisk—if you're looking for an upper body workout). A full-sized blender will be too large to create the right kind of emulsification for this small batch.

YIELD: ⁷⁄₈ CUP

$\frac{1}{2}$ cup dried, crumbled herb or spice

1 egg yolk

2 teaspoons lemon juice

1 teaspoon water

$\frac{3}{4}$ cup olive oil

Grind the dried herb or spice into a powder, and transfer it to a small food processor or a bowl or container just large enough to fit a hand blender. The blades need to make good contact with the ingredients, which is why a small batch in a big blender won't work.

Add the egg yolk, lemon juice, and water to the powdered herb or spice and combine with the hand blender or food processor. *Slowly* drizzle the oil into the egg mixture, continuing to blend. If you rush this step, you will not get the necessary emulsification.

You should notice the mixture beginning to thicken once half of the oil is incorporated. At this point, you can drizzle the oil in a little more quickly, but make sure it's no more than a slow stream.

When you've finished adding the oil, check the texture of the mayonnaise. Does it feel like store-bought mayonnaise? If the answer is yes, congratulations! If the answer is no, continue to blend a little longer, until the mayonnaise has thickened up to the right consistency.

The mayonnaise will keep, refrigerated, for 5–7 days.

WILD GINGERSNAPS
WITH JUNIPER BERRY ICING

If you already have a favorite gingersnap recipe, feel free to use that, substituting wild ginger for tropical ginger and spicebush berries for the traditional gingersnap spices. The first time my sister Sarah tasted these, she said, "They're like champagne!" and I knew exactly what she meant. They are light, fancy, and exciting.

YIELD: 50 TO 70 GINGERSNAPS

FOR THE COOKIES
1 stick unsalted butter, softened

1²⁄₃ cups sugar

¼ teaspoon vanilla extract

1 egg

¹⁄₆ cup molasses

1¹⁄₂ cups all-purpose flour

1¹⁄₄ teaspoons baking soda

¼ teaspoon salt

1 tablespoon ground, dried spicebush berries

2¹⁄₂ teaspoons ground, dried ginger rhizomes

FOR THE ICING
¹⁄₃ cup juniper berries

³⁄₄ cup half-and-half

1 pound confectioners' sugar

Cream together the butter and sugar. Add the vanilla and egg and beat until fluffy.

Add the molasses and blend well. Then, add the flour, baking soda, salt, ground spicebush berries, and dried ginger rhizomes, and mix until just combined.

Spread a sheet of parchment paper or cling film (about 18 inches long) on the counter and transfer the dough to the paper or cling film. Form the dough into a snake and wrap it up. Roll it around a little to get rid of any air pockets. Close up the ends of the wrapping and freeze the dough overnight or until it's solid.

When you're ready to bake, preheat the oven to 350°F.

Unwrap the dough and slice it as thinly as possible, aiming for medallions that are ⅛ inch thick. Lay the cookies out on the baking sheet, leaving about an inch between each one. Bake for 8–9 minutes, then let them cool on the baking sheet before transferring to a plate. The cookies will still be soft when they come out of the oven, and they need the cooling time to become crisp.

continued

If you bake the cookies in batches, return the dough to the freezer in between. If the dough warms up, the cookies will still taste great, but they'll spread much more during baking and you'll end up with one giant gingersnap.

To make the icing, use a mortar and pestle to lightly crush the juniper berries. You may also use a spice grinder, but don't go overboard. You don't want a powder, you just want to break the berries up a little. Exposing more surface area makes it easier to infuse the juniper flavor into the cream.

Combine the berries and half-and-half in a saucepan and heat, whisking to avoid scorching. Remove the liquid from the heat at the first sign of bubbles forming around the edge of the liquid, then allow it to steep and cool for 4–5 hours. Let the pan cool to room temperature in the kitchen, then move it to the refrigerator to continue steeping.

Strain the half-and-half and discard the berries.

Measure the confectioners' sugar into a bowl, then stir in the half-and-half, bit by bit, until the icing reaches the desired consistency. You may not need the whole ¾ cup, but you'll probably come close. Transfer the icing to a squeeze bottle, a pastry bag, or a Ziploc bag with the corner snipped off and drizzle the icing in patterns, or frost your cookies with a spatula. Extra icing will keep in the refrigerator for several weeks.

FILÉ GUMBO

I don't like okra. It's not the mucilage, it's the flavor. Fortunately, okra isn't necessary for an authentic gumbo, although it's often used to thicken this soup. The original filé is powdered, dried sassafras leaves, and that's what I use to thicken and flavor my gumbo. Sassafras leaves have a citrusy flavor that is delicious in this dish. Harvest your fresh leaves mid-summer or later to get more thickening power out of them.

The hardest part of making this recipe is making the roux. I was intimidated before I started and, sure enough, I blew it on my first try. I'd read that you had to watch the roux like a hawk and that it would be immediately clear when it burned. Well, I *did* watch it like a hawk and it *was* immediately clear it had burned. Try making yours over medium-low heat and stop when the color resembles that of peanut butter. I hope that helps. Since that first dismal failure, it has worked well for me.

YIELD: 6 TO 8 SERVINGS

½ cup peanut oil

½ cup all-purpose flour

1 red, 1 orange, and 1 yellow bell pepper, chopped into bite-sized pieces

1 large onion, chopped into bite-sized pieces

1 teaspoon black pepper

½ teaspoon cayenne pepper

1 tablespoon ground celery seed

1 tablespoon ground bee balm

1 teaspoon salt

3 bay leaves

6 cups stock or water

12 ounces of sausage of choice, cut into bite-sized pieces

1 pound small shrimp, peeled

1½ cups chopped dock greens

Filé powder, to taste

Cooked white rice

Heat a heavy-bottomed pan and pour in the oil and flour. Whisk constantly as the flour browns. Don't look away. Keep the heat on medium-low and remove the pan from the heat *as soon as* it has reached the right color (a light peanut-butter brown). If it smells even the tiniest bit burnt, throw out the roux and start over.

Add the bell peppers and onion to the roux and stir for 5 minutes to soften the vegetables. Yes, constant stirring is required. It's worth it, you'll see.

Add the black and cayenne peppers, the celery seed, bee balm, salt, and bay leaves, stirring to combine well.

Next, add the liquid. I had a quart of lobster stock on hand, so I used that plus 2 cups of water. A blend of chicken stock and water would also have been fine. Bring the mixture to a boil, add the sausage, and reduce the heat to a simmer, cooking for 30 minutes.

Add the shrimp and dock, then simmer for another 5 minutes. The dock greens not only add flavor, they also help thicken the gumbo (see page 82).

At this point, many recipes ask you to add the filé powder and simmer for another few minutes. Do not do this. Instead, serve the gumbo, place a shaker or small saucer of filé on the table, and allow each person to add their own, thickening the broth according to their own personal preference.

Add rice and enjoy.

Yucca blossoms

FLOWERS

· ·

We've all seen flower petals used to garnish a plate or glass, but this chapter isn't about that. Sure, pretty is nice—you'll find a few recipes in this section chosen for their appearance and novelty—but most focus on buds and blooms with substantial flavor.

Most edible flowers are on the sweet side, getting their flavor from nectar and natural yeasts. But some flowers are surprisingly savory, and still others have different flavors depending on when they're harvested. For example, immature milkweed florets are a savory ingredient, while fully ripe milkweed flowers taste sweet.

And speaking of milkweed . . . before you harvest all the flowers from a plant, ask yourself if you'll want to pick fruit from it later in the season. Young milkweed pods are a tasty vegetable, and if you harvest all the milkweed flowers, you won't get any pods. The same is true for rose hips, plums, elderberries, and yucca fruit (all of which you will meet in chapter four).

Not to worry, because you can eat your flowers and still have fruit! The easiest way is to limit your flower harvest. Leave half of the flowers behind to be pollinated and fertilized, and they will produce fruit. Alternatively, if you're harvesting rose or yucca petals, you can carefully remove the flower petals, leaving the pistil and stamens behind for pollination, fertilization, and fruit formation. Of course, flower petals are often what attract the pollinators to your plants, so harvesting this way will probably reduce your fruit crop.

It's important to time your foraging correctly when it comes to flowers; they are a delicate and ephemeral harvest. If you want to capture the natural yeasts found in the pollen, gather after several warm, sunny days. Rain washes away pollen, and you may not get the flavor or fermentation you desire. If you hope to capture the sweetness of a flower's nectar, harvest in the morning, after the sun is warm but before it gets so hot that the nectar dries up or has been ferried away by pollinators. Early morning is also best for harvesting petals that will be consumed fresh.

A good general rule is that if a plant is considered edible, and if its flowers have a strong scent, then the flower has flavor and is worth eating. But this isn't a hard and fast rule. There are some plants for which only the flowers are edible and all other parts are toxic (I'll point out these exceptions!), and others where flowers are safe to eat but have almost no scent or flavor.

Preserving the Harvest

Preserving flowers is trickier than preserving many other plant parts. Their flavors are usually more delicate than those of spices, fruit, or greens, and many of the flowers themselves are quite fragile. You'll get the most flavor out of your flowers by using them fresh. That being said, here are a few ways to preserve your flower harvests for later use.

DEHYDRATION

Drying works for flowers with strong scents and colors. The dried orange petals of the common daylily can be crumbled or ground into a powder and used to color rice or pasta. (I know I promised to focus on taste over looks, but the orange color you get from daylily petals is pretty spectacular.) Dried elderflowers, milkweed flowers, fragrant rose petals, and pineapple weed can be rehydrated and used to make teas and syrups. Their scent and flavor will be different from their fresh flavors, but they're worth preserving if you have an especially bountiful harvest.

FREEZING

I was once told that dandelion flowers couldn't be frozen—that they'd continue to mature and turn to fluff in your freezer. Of course I had to try it anyway, primarily because picking dandelion petals for dandelion wine is so tedious that I never managed to process enough in a single sitting. Turns out, you *can* freeze dandelion flowers and they *don't* turn to fluff in the freezer. Just be sure to separate the petals from the calyces[1] before freezing, because when thawed they will be soft and much more difficult to handle.

Freezing delicate flowers pretty much destroys their texture. This isn't a big deal if you're making wine or a syrup, but if you want to enjoy the mouthfeel of the flower, freezing is not the best way to go. Substantial buds, like savory white top mustard florets or immature milkweed flowers, freeze well. Blanch them in boiling water to stop the ripening process, shock them in ice water (to stop the cooking process), and freeze in one-cup batches. I vacuum seal any batches that I plan to store for more than a month.

PICKLING

I like pickles, but most of the time, whatever you pickle ends up tasting more like the brine than the original ingredient. Which, when it comes to your

---

1. Calyces is the plural of calyx. The calyx is the green collar that holds the petals of some flowers together, and in the case of dandelions, it has a bitter flavor that you don't want to include in whatever you're making.

hard-earned foraged harvests, seems like a waste of flavor to me. Additionally, most flowers don't stand up well (texturally) to being canned, so if you *do* decide to pickle flowers or flower buds, use a refrigerator pickle recipe rather than one that requires a boiling water bath. Mustard flowers can be added to traditional pickles for sharp, horseradishy flavor, and daylily buds can be pickled in any brine you like, sweet or spicy.

Seasonal Availability

Flowers are primarily a spring and summer harvest, although in certain parts of the country, they may bloom in fall and winter.

Black locust (*Robinia pseudoacacia*) and New Mexican locust (*R. neomexicana*) flowers are both beautiful and sweet, with a floral flavor that has undertones of grape. They bloom in hanging clusters, making it easy to harvest a lot in a short amount of time. But watch out for the thorny branches—these trees are armed! Locust flowers are best used fresh, but they can be frozen for infusing in alcohol, cream, or water.

The immature male flowers of cattails (*Typha* spp.) have a barely sweet, corn-like flavor. Male and female flowers are encased in a green sheath at the top of a tall, narrow flower stem. The flower stalk is three to six inches long,

	Spring	Summer	Fall	Winter
black or New Mexico locust flowers (*Robinia* spp.)	X	X		
cattail (immature male flowers) (*Typha* spp.)	X	X		
dandelion (*Taraxacum* spp.)	X	X	X	X
daylily (*Hemerocallis fulva*)	X	X		
elderflowers (*Sambucus* spp.)	X	X		
Japanese honeysuckle (*Lonicera japonica*)	X	X		
magnolia (*Magnolia* spp.)	X		X	X
milkweed buds & flowers (*Asclepias* spp.)	X	X		
mustard buds & flowers (various species)	X			
pineapple weed (*Matricaria discoidea*)		X	X	
plum blossoms (*Prunus* spp.)	X			
Queen Anne's lace (*Daucus carota*)		X	X	
redbud flowers (*Cercis* spp.)	X			
rose (*Rosa* spp.)	X	X	X	
yucca flowers (*Yucca* spp.)		X		

shaped like a narrow cigar, with male flowers located at the top of the stalk and female flowers underneath. There is a clear dividing line between the male and female sections of the stalk. Harvest the flowers when they are still sheathed. If the male flowers have started to open, they will show bright yellow pollen. You want to harvest them before that happens.

To harvest, you can snip off either the entire flower or just the male portion, right at the dividing line. Bring them home, rinse, then steam the flowers for about 10 minutes. Once they're cool enough to handle, use a fork or your fingers to remove the male flowers from around the thin midrib to which they cling. Cattail flowers are best used fresh, and the season is short, so keep an eye out!

Dandelion (*Taraxacum* spp.) flowers may be the most familiar flower on the block. The blooms are sunny and bright, but I'll be honest: they don't have a ton of flavor. Syrups and jellies made from dandelion flowers are pretty but generically sweet. I include them here for several reasons: 1) Everybody recognizes them, which makes them distinctly nonthreatening to forage for, 2) there is no danger of overharvesting this ubiquitous plant, and 3) kids love them. If you're looking for a kitchen project to try with your kids, dandelions are a lot of fun. For sweet applications, use only dandelion petals; these can be preserved by freezing. If you're making a savory fritter, you may use the whole, fresh flower head.

There are hundreds of cultivars of daylilies, but I can only guarantee that the orange ditch lily (*Hemerocallis fulva*) is edible. The lemon daylily (*H. lilioasphodelus*) is also known to be edible, but I have never tried it. Even if you find an edible species, there is a caveat. A small percentage of people are allergic to this plant and may suffer varying degrees of GI upset after consuming any part of it. Of all the foragers I know (and I know a lot!), two people have this problem. So please, the first time you try it, consume only a small quantity. The unopened flower buds can be prepared like green beans, and the dried flower petals add excellent color to rice dishes. Fresh flower petals can be added to salads for a burst of orange.

The pollen of elderflowers (*Sambucus* spp.) contains yeast that ferments naturally when combined with sugar and water. If you want to use elderflowers for a natural soda, harvest after several dry, sunny days, since rain washes away the pollen and yeast. Only the flowers and fruit of the elderberry are edible; all other parts of the plant are toxic to humans. The flowers may be preserved by drying, but they are more flavorful when used fresh. If you hope to harvest fruit in late summer, be sure to leave some elderflowers on the plant to be pollinated.

Is there anyone who hasn't sucked the sweet nectar out of a Japanese honeysuckle (*Lonicera japonica*) blossom? Not all honeysuckle flowers are edible, but Japanese honeysuckle is the most common species and is considered invasive in many states, particularly on the East Coast. Its flowers make a delicate syrup. Japanese honeysuckle blooms should be used fresh.

There are over 200 species of magnolia (*Magnolia* spp.), and not all are equally delicious, so nibble a petal before you harvest a bunch. (I haven't tasted every one yet, but I'm working on it.) My favorite are the flowers of the saucer magnolia (*Magnolia × soulangeana*). Their flavor is warm and spicy. In contrast, I find the petals of star magnolia (*Magnolia stellata*) to be bitter and unappealing. The pistils and stamens are also flavorful and can be included in your recipe. Magnolia petals are best used fresh.

Milkweed buds (*Asclepias syriaca, A. speciosa*) are little round clusters of green-beany goodness. Harvest the tightly closed buds and use them fresh, or blanch and freeze them for long-term storage. Milkweed buds can be sautéed and served as a vegetable or added to soups, quiches, and stir-fries. Fully ripe, open flowers are full of sweet nectar and make an excellent syrup, jelly, or shrub.[2] Dried mature milkweed flowers have a strong, sweet fragrance and can be used in tea blends. There are many species of milkweed, but the two listed above are the only species I can promise you are fully edible.

Mustard flowers come in many shapes, colors, and sizes, but they all have several things in common. They are savory, not sweet. They have four petals arranged in a cross formation. They have six stamens, two short and four long. You'll find a wide range of flavors among mustards, from the mild and earthy musk mustard (*Chorispora tenella*) to the sharp and biting London rocket (*Sisymbrium irio*). The unripe buds of whitetop mustard (*Lepidium draba*) look like mini broccoli (a cousin!) and make a substantial vegetable. Their flavor is well preserved by blanching and freezing. Many mustards are highly invasive, so feel free to harvest those in quantity and stock up that freezer.

Pineapple weed (*Matricaria discoidea*) is a little weed with a lot of flavor. Its flowers are small and have no petals—just a rounded, yellow mound of disc

---

2. Shrub is another word for a drinking vinegar. You'll find a recipe on page 55.

flowers.[3] Crush one between your fingers and you'll be rewarded with a distinct pineapple smell. Fresh flowers can be eaten raw in salads or infused in cream, sugar, and alcohol. I've harvested this plant from Florida to the Arctic Circle—it literally grows almost everywhere. Dried flowers, though less flavorful than fresh flowers, can be used for tea.

Plum blossoms (*Prunus* spp.) are exceptionally fragrant, and that fragrance transfers well to sugar and cream. You may use any fragrant plum blossoms, from the shrubby native American plum (*P. americana*) to the common purple-leaf plum (*P. cerasifera*) that's often planted as a street tree. And since flowers are usually borne in great abundance, it's easy to harvest enough to cook with and leave plenty behind to form fruit. Plum blossoms should be used fresh. They'll keep in the fridge for several days while you gather enough to work with.

Queen Anne's lace (*Daucus carota*) flowers can be used to make a naturally fermented soda or a Juicy Fruit–flavored jelly. Some people claim they get a pink jelly, but I never have. Mine is pretty and tasty, but definitely not pink. I tell you that not so you'll feel sorry for me, but so you'll know you're not alone if the same thing happens to you. Use Queen Anne's lace flowers fresh.

Redbud (*Cercis* spp.) flowers add a brilliant flash of magenta (there *are* white-flowered species, but why?) and a sweet pop of texture to salads and crudité platters. You can also add them to muffins and quick breads, but they lose their color when baked or heated. Mix them into pasta, chicken, or tuna salad or sprinkle them on top of ice cream as a surprising garnish. Some people make redbud jelly, which is pretty, but tastes indefinably sweet to me. Redbud flowers may be picked when tightly closed or fully open. They should be used fresh.

Rose (*Rosa* spp.) petals are only worth harvesting if they are fragrant. A rose with no scent is a rose with no flavor. *R. multiflora* is classified as invasive, prohibited, or a noxious weed in many states, so feel free to harvest liberally. Its flowers have excellent scent and flavor. Dried petals can be used for teas and maintain their scent and flavor better than most delicate flowers. Colorful rose petals add flash to a dish, although cooking mutes the brightness.

Yucca (*Yucca* spp.) flowers are a traditional food in Latin America, where they are often cooked with eggs. I haven't tasted every species, although they

---

3. Flowers in the daisy family (*Asteraceae*) are composed of ray flowers (aka petals) and disc flowers (small round flowers that make up the center of the bloom).

MAKE YOUR OWN ROSE WATER

Distilling your own rose water is surprisingly easy. Place a small ovenproof ramekin upside down in the middle of a large pasta pot on your stove. Spread four cups of rose petals around the bottom of the pot, circling the ramekin. Next, add four cups of water to the rose petals in the pot. The water level should not be higher than the top of the ramekin.

Place a wide-mouth two-cup measuring cup on top of the ramekin. Cover the pot with the lid turned upside down. Turn on the heat, and when the water begins to boil, reduce to keep the liquid at a low simmer.

Place a bag of ice cubes on top of the inverted pot lid.

As the water turns to steam, it volatilizes the essential oils in the rose petals. The steam rises, then condenses when it hits the ice-cooled lid of the pot. The inverted lid funnels the water to drip into the measuring cup. And that condensed water contains the fragrance and taste of the rose petals.

Check the rose petals every 10 minutes. The most concentrated fragrance and flavor will be produced during the first 20 minutes. After 40 minutes, the petals will have lost their color and it's time to stop boiling. Let everything cool, then pour the rose water from the measuring cup into a jar or bottle. The rose water will keep in the refrigerator for up to 6 months.

are all generally considered edible. Some people get an itchy throat when eating the flowers raw, and some people eat only the petals, not the pistils and stamens inside. I eat the whole flower, both raw and cooked, with no trouble at all. Yucca flowers should be used fresh or quickly blanched and frozen for storage. Frozen yucca flowers can be used in sautés, soups, and stews, but will not have the correct texture for stuffing (see Stuffed Yucca Flowers on page 73).

General Techniques

You've harvested your flowers, and since most are best used fresh, you don't have time to mess around! Let's get you started with some general techniques to turn those blooms into delicious food.

SUGARS & SYRUPS

Flavored sugars can be used for baking or to sweeten a cup of tea. They're best made with flowers that hold their scent when dried, like rose petals, elderflowers, and milkweed flowers. Combine 1 part sugar with ½ part dried flower petals in a food processor, pulverize, and store in a container with a tight-fitting lid.

Simple syrups are an excellent way to preserve flower flavors, and they're great ingredients to have on hand for cocktails, desserts, and marinades. Begin by combining equal parts sugar and flowers. Let this sit, covered, for 24 hours. Transfer the mixture to a sauté pan and add an equal part water. Whisk to combine until the sugar has fully dissolved, then remove the pan from the heat, cover, and let it sit for another 24 hours. Strain off the solids and transfer the liquid to a container with a tight-fitting lid. This will last up to four weeks in the fridge or at least a year if canned in a boiling water bath for ten minutes.

ALCOHOL

To infuse alcohol with the color and flavor of your favorite edible flower, combine equal parts (by volume) flowers and vodka in a closed container and give it a shake. Let it sit, then taste after 24 hours. If the flavor isn't strong enough, let it sit for another day or two. When you taste-test, you should be able to smell the flavoring ingredient as you bring the vodka to your mouth and be able to taste that ingredient through the alcohol.

When the vodka has been sufficiently flavored, strain off the solids and bottle the liquid.

You might also experiment with other base spirits. Both locust flowers and milkweed flowers are tasty (and lovely) infused in gin. Magnolia-infused bourbon makes a very special julep.

CREAM

Some flower flavors infuse well in cream, which can then be whipped into a flavored whipped cream or used as the base for ice cream, panna cotta, and puddings. Cold cream infusions are made by steeping the foraged ingredient in cream for 24–48 hours in the refrigerator. They take longer than hot infusions and are often worth the wait, producing brighter flavors than hot infusions. I recommend a cold infusion for elderflowers, plum blossoms, milkweed flowers, pineapple weed, roses, and honeysuckle.

Hot infusions can be completed in under an hour and work well for stronger flavors, like magnolia flowers. To make a hot infusion, heat (but don't boil) the foraged ingredient in the cream, then turn off the heat, cover the pan, and allow the liquid to cool for an hour before straining off the solids. Feel free to try both methods with your favorite flavors and decide for yourself which one you prefer.

VINEGAR

Drinking vinegars (aka shrubs) are a great way to preserve the flavor of flowers and fruits. In fact, in the days before refrigeration, vinegar prevented bacterial and fungal growth and allowed people to enjoy perishable flavors out of season. Shrubs start with shrub syrups, which can be made hot or cold. Hot shrub syrups come together quickly, while cold shrub syrups take several days. Both should be allowed to age for at least a month before using. They really do get better with time.

To make a cold flower shrub, combine equal parts flowers and sugar, mix well, and cover, letting the sugar sit at room temperature overnight. The next day, add an equal part vinegar and stir well. (For flower shrubs, I recommend using vinegar with a delicate flavor, like white wine or champagne vinegar. Apple cider vinegar brings its own flavor to the party.) Let this sit, covered, at room temperature for 48 hours, giving it a shake occasionally to help the sugar dissolve. Strain off the solids, transfer the liquid to a jar or bottle with a tight-fitting lid, and store in the refrigerator. You can taste the shrub syrup now, but the flavor will be less sharp and more interesting after a month or two in the fridge.

If you're pressed for time, you can make a faster hot version by combining equal parts sugar and vinegar in a sauté pan, heating and whisking to dissolve the sugar. Add the flowers, let the mixture cool, then strain off the solids. Transfer the shrub syrup to a jar or bottle and store in the refrigerator.

Shrubs have a strong vinegar flavor, and a little goes a long way. Use one tablespoon to flavor six ounces of seltzer or water, or try a teaspoon with your favorite spirit. You can play with the proportions until you discover what suits your taste buds.

STUFFED FLOWERS

Some flowers are substantial enough to be used as vessels. You'll find a savory stuffed yucca flower recipe at the end of this chapter, but an easier, no-cook way to use flowers is to remove the pistils and stamens and stuff the body of the flower with an herbed cheese. This works well with larger flowers like daylilies. You could also place the empty flower in a small glass dish, then fill it with ice cream. Just saying.

BUTTERMILK MUFFINS

Some flowers have more flavor than others, but all of them are pretty and many of them also add texture. Flowers like redbuds and locust blooms can be used whole and add a nice crunch. Magnolia petals, honeysuckle flowers, and rose petals should be roughly chopped into bite-sized pieces. Dandelion petals can be added to the batter whole.

I suggest a simple muffin batter for this recipe so you can taste and see the foraged flowers in the batter. Of course, you can spice things up if you like, but try the recipe as is first to get a feel for your ingredients. This recipe can easily be doubled.

YIELD: 6 MUFFINS

1 cup all-purpose flour

1 teaspoon baking powder

1/2 teaspoon baking soda

1/2 cup buttermilk

3 tablespoons honey

1 egg

1/4 cup melted butter

1/2 cup foraged flowers (prepared as described above)

Preheat the oven to 375°F and grease the muffin tin.

In a bowl, whisk together the dry ingredients and set aside.

In another bowl, combine the wet ingredients, then add these to the dry ingredients and mix well to combine. Fold in the flowers or petals to distribute them evenly throughout the batter.

Spoon the batter into 6 muffin cups. Each cup should be about ⅔ full.

Bake for 15 minutes, or until the edges of the muffins are golden brown and a knife inserted into the middle of a muffin comes out clean. Allow the muffins to cool for 10 minutes in the tin, then turn them out and let them cool completely.

NOTE: If you make this recipe with dandelions, you won't get a lot of flavor. But the petals add some sweetness, and it's fun to be able to show your kids (and adult friends) that they can eat dandelions.

SAVORY QUICHE

I originally made this with green milkweed florets, but mustard flowers, yucca blossoms, daylily buds, redbud flowers, and dandelion petals also work well. If you use milkweed or daylily buds, you'll want to break them up into bite-sized pieces before cooking.

Only milkweed florets require blanching. This is to remove the milky sap. All other flowers and buds listed here can be used raw. If you make this with mustard flowers, yucca blossoms, redbud flowers, or dandelion petals, whisk them in with the egg mixture and pour into the pie crust. If you make the quiche with daylily buds, roughly chop them into bite-sized pieces and place them on the crust before pouring over the egg mixture.

YIELD: 1 QUICHE

1½ cups milkweed florets

1 pie crust

4 eggs

1 cup plain Greek yogurt

1 tablespoon field garlic powder

1 teaspoon salt

½ teaspoon pepper

1 teaspoon dried, crumbled bee balm leaves or flowers

½ cup grated or crumbled cheese (feta, cheddar, and mozzarella all work well)

Preheat the oven to 375°F.

Blanch the milkweed florets in boiling water until they turn bright green, 2–5 minutes. Drain the florets and shock them in ice water to stop the cooking process.

Place the pie crust (store-bought or homemade) in an 8-inch pie pan and crimp the edges.

Whisk together the eggs, yogurt, garlic powder, salt, pepper, and bee balm in a bowl. Spread the blanched milkweed florets on top of the pie crust, then pour the egg mixture over them.

Sprinkle the grated cheese on top and bake for 30 minutes or until the egg mixture is solid.

This quiche can be served for breakfast, lunch, or dinner, and it's tasty warm or at room temperature.

NOTE: Let's get this out of the way now. I don't make my own pie crusts and I'm not ashamed to say it. I'd rather spend my time foraging than waiting for pie crust dough to chill, and besides, store-bought pie crusts are pretty darned good. Go ahead and judge me if you want, but it's not going to change my mind.

FLOWER FRITTERS

Let's face it: fritters mostly taste like sugar and fried dough. Those are tasty things, but they do obscure the flavor of your foraged ingredients. Still, they're fun to make and a great way to get kids interested in wild foods. The recipe works best with substantial, fresh flower clusters like honey locust and elderflowers. If you'd like to use smaller flowers in fritters, I suggest adding them to your favorite pancake batter.

Dandelion flowers make a nice savory fritter. When harvesting, be sure to leave some stem in place to use as a handle. Substitute ¼ cup breadcrumbs for ¼ cup of the flour and instead of dusting with confectioners' sugar, sprinkle your fritters with mushroom powder, sumac powder, or a flavored salt.

This is the simplest fritter batter you could possibly make, and that's intentional. I want you to taste the underlying flowers. Getting the texture right is important, and this requires a large temperature difference between the hot oil and cold batter. Refrigerate the batter for a half hour before dipping and frying the flower clusters.

YIELD: 4 TO 6 SERVINGS

1 cup self-rising flour	Vegetable oil
1 cup unflavored seltzer	Confectioners' sugar, to taste
2 cups flower clusters with stems, loosely packed	

Combine the flour and seltzer in a bowl and whisk to combine until the batter is smooth. Refrigerate for 30 minutes.

Gather the flower clusters. You will want approximately 2 cups, but it depends on the flower being used. Dandelions will use more batter, elderflowers will use less, and honey locust will be somewhere in between. Shake the flowers to get rid of any insect hitchhikers. Unless the clusters are very dirty (and why would they be?), don't wash them. There's a lot of flavor in the pollen and you want to hold onto that.

Heat the oil in a pan or deep fryer. You'll need it to be at least an inch deep. The temperature is right when the tip of a wooden skewer placed in the oil starts to sizzle.

Using the stem of the flower cluster as a handle, dip the cluster in the batter and place it in the hot oil. Let it fry until light golden brown, then remove the fritter and put it on a paper towel to absorb a little oil. You'll probably be able to fit several fritters in the oil at once, but don't crowd them so much that they stick together.

Sprinkle a dusting of confectioners' sugar onto the fritters and serve them warm. It's fine to eat the small individual stems that attach each flower to the cluster, but don't eat the main stem of the cluster that you used for a dipping handle. Not only is the big stem not delicious, but the large stem of the elderflower cluster may cause GI upset. The flowers and small stems are perfectly safe.

NOTE: If you don't have self-rising flower, you can substitute with 1 cup all-purpose flour, 1½ teaspoons baking powder, and ¼ teaspoon salt, thoroughly combining them before use.

FLOWER SODA

Flower sodas work because the naturally occurring yeasts in some flower pollens allow fermentation to take place without adding artificial carbonation. That being said, you can also make a soda by adding seltzer to any flower syrup. But if you want to make a naturally fermented flower soda, the best candidates are Queen Anne's lace, elderflower, and milkweed flowers. The color of milkweed soda is almost too beautiful to be believed.

This recipe makes four quarts. You can make a half batch, or simply scale it according to how many flowers you find. Don't be afraid to get creative. If you don't have a lime or lemon, try orange or grapefruit peels.

I use plastic soda bottles sterilized with a 10% bleach solution to store my finished soda, but you can use quart jars or swing top glass bottles if that's what you have on hand. The important thing is that you must be able to release the gas regularly, as fermentation continues. Otherwise, you will have an explosive experience. And not in a good way.

YIELD: 4 QUARTS

5 cups milkweed flowers	12 cups water
4 cups sugar	2 limes or lemons, peel only

Snip the milkweed flowers off their stems and move them to a large pot or container. It's ok to include the slim, individual flower stems, but you don't want the thick stem of the umbel.[4]

Add the sugar, water, and lime peels, stirring to dissolve the sugar. Cover the container with a dish towel or cheesecloth and leave it on the kitchen counter at room temperature. Ideally, you'd give this a stir every day to aerate the liquid and speed fermentation. However, life (in my experience) is rarely ideal, and when I had to leave town mid-soda-making, I fastened the cheesecloth to the top of the container with an elastic band and hoped for the best. Five days later I came home to a wonderfully fermenting brew, so yay!

---

4. An umbel is a flower cluster composed of small flowers attached by individual stems to a central point.

continued

You'll know your soda is fermenting when a quick stir produces visible and audible bubbles. If you're not sure, wait another day; you shouldn't need more than 5–7 days.

Strain off the solids, pressing on them to release as much liquid as possible, then transfer the liquid into your sterilized bottles or jars. Leave a few inches of air space at the top of each bottle and screw on the tops firmly. If you're using plastic, squeeze the bottles to feel how flexible they are; this will be helpful later. Leave the closed bottles or jars on the counter.

As the soda ferments, it produces carbon dioxide, which builds up pressure in the bottles and forces the gas to dissolve into the liquid. The pressurized gas will be released as fizzy bubbles when the bottle is opened. One of the reasons I like to ferment in plastic is that you can feel how fermentation is progressing.

Check the bottles every day, gently squeezing on their sides. When they are rock hard (no give at all beneath your fingers), they're ready to be drunk. You can either move them to the refrigerator for immediate consumption or keep them cool and dark until you're ready. But since this recipe includes no preservatives, don't wait more than a week or two.

NOTE: If you make this with Queen Anne's lace or elderflowers, use 20 flower clusters and one thinly sliced lemon instead of the citrus peel.

AVOID AN EXPLOSION

Pressure continues to build as the bottles sit. Left untended, they may explode, even in a cool, dark basement. Now's your chance to learn from my experience: once the bottles have reached the rock-hard state, leak a little gas from them at regular intervals. Loosen the cap for about three seconds, just long enough to hear gas escape. Then tighten the cap and notice that you can once again feel a little give in the bottle (if you're using plastic). After a few days, the bottle is rock hard again, and it's time to repeat the process. Take this precaution and you'll be explosion-free.

When it's time to open a bottle, remember, there's a lot of carbonation in there. Crack the bottle open just a smidge and let it sit in the sink while it bubbles up and some gas escapes. Once the bubbles recede a bit, you're ready to pour. Some particles may settle out of the liquid, so pour gently to avoid stirring up the sediment.

FLOWER LIQUEURS

If you've already made a flower syrup and a flower vodka infusion, most of your work is done! If not, go ahead and do both of those things, then come back here for instructions on how to finish up.

YIELD: 1 BEVERAGE

1 part Spice Syrups (page 29)

1 part flower vodka infusion (see page 54)

Combine equal parts flower syrup and vodka infusion to make a liqueur. Because alcohol and water release different flavor compounds, the resulting liqueur will be more flavorful and complex than either liquid on its own. Sip your liqueur over ice for a sophisticated dessert drink, mixed with seltzer for a refreshing spritzer, or in a creative craft cocktail. Or, make up a big batch, bottle it, and keep it in the fridge to have on hand for when you want to impress your friends and family.

My favorite foraged flower liqueurs are plum blossom, pineapple weed, and magnolia flower. The plum combines well with a fizzy sake, and the pineapple weed goes great with coconut water. Try substituting magnolia flower liqueur for the bourbon in your next mint julep.

FLOWER CREAM CAKE

This recipe works well with plum blossoms, rose petals, and magnolia flowers. Be sure to save some fresh petals to use as garnish. Remember, we also eat with our eyes!

YIELD: 1 CAKE

2 cups clean flowers or petals, roughly chopped

2 cups cream

3/4 cup sugar

1 1/2 cups all-purpose flour

2 teaspoons baking powder

2 eggs, room temperature

Confectioners' sugar, to taste

Rinse the flowers, then roughly chop into pieces about an inch square. If you're using magnolia flowers, the pistils and stamens are just as flavorful as the petals, so no need to remove them. You may also use whole plum flowers, but with roses, use only the petals.

In a heavy saucepan, combine the cream and flowers. Heat the liquid gently, whisking occasionally to avoid scorching. You don't want to boil the cream. When bubbles begin to appear around the edge of the saucepan, reduce the heat and barely simmer for 25 minutes. Strain the cream and throw away the flowers. You'll use this infused cream both in the cake and for the icing.

Preheat the oven to 350°F and coat the inside of a small Bundt pan with nonstick baking spray. This recipe is intended for a 3-cup Bundt pan, but if you have a 6-cup Bundt pan, you can use that. Just note that the cake will be shorter and cook more quickly.

Combine the sugar, flour, and baking powder in a mixing bowl, and whisk together. Add ⅔ cup of the infused cream and the eggs, whisking to remove all lumps.

Pour the batter into the greased pan, and bake until the cake is golden brown and a toothpick inserted in the center of the cake comes out clean. In a full-size pan, start checking at 30 minutes. In a 3-cup pan, start checking at 40 minutes.

Remove the cake from the oven and allow it to cool for 10–15 minutes before turning it out onto a plate.

While the cake cools, assemble your icing. Transfer the remainder of the infused cream to a small bowl and add confectioners' sugar, 1 tablespoon at a time. Whisk after each addition until the icing reaches the desired consistency. It should be liquid enough to pour onto the warm cake, but not so thin that it slides right off. Don't skimp on the icing! Because this is a simple cake and the icing is flower-flavored, you want it in every bite.

Serve the cake warm or at room temperature.

CUSTARD

Custards are easier than flans, because you don't have to tip them out of their dishes to reveal a perfectly caramelized layer of sugar on top. Which is not to say you shouldn't try, but starting with custard is easier and may give you the courage to try a flan down the line. Flans are made with more eggs/yolks than custards, which gives them a stronger structure and makes it easier for them to stand up on their own. If you'd like to try a flan, go ahead and infuse the cream according to the instructions below, then use it in place of the unflavored cream in your favorite flan recipe.

This recipe can easily be doubled. It works well with fragrant rose petals, plum blossoms, milkweed flowers, and pineapple weed.

YIELD: 2 (4-OUNCE) SERVINGS

1 cup whole milk	2 tablespoons sugar
1 cup cleaned, fragrant flowers	Pinch of salt
1 extra large egg	

Combine the milk and flowers in a saucepan and gradually bring the milk to a simmer, whisking to prevent scorching. Allow the milk to barely simmer for 5 minutes, whisking constantly, then remove the pan from the heat, cover, and let the flowers steep for 30 minutes.

Strain off the solids, pressing down on them to release every possible drop of liquid. Throw away the flowers, then pour the infused milk through a fine strainer (like a yogurt strainer or gold coffee filter) to remove any solids that may have snuck through the first time.

Preheat the oven to 325°F.

Whisk the egg, then combine it with the infused milk, sugar, and salt.

Pour the custard into individual dishes, then place those dishes in a large baking pan and fill the pan with hot water until it reaches halfway up the custard dishes. The water moderates the heat of the oven, and both custards and flans have more delicate textures when they bake gently.

Bake the custards for 40–50 minutes, depending on the size of the dishes. (Start checking at 30 minutes.) The custards should be jiggly, but a knife inserted in the center should come out clean.

Remove the dishes from the hot water bath and let them cool on the counter for about an hour. Then cover the dishes and refrigerate until you're ready to serve. Top your custard with a few tablespoons of foraged flower simple syrup (see page 54) for an extra blast of unbuyable flavor.

HERE'S A TIP I wish I'd read before I started on my custard/flan journey: When combining your ingredients, be thorough but *gentle*. A heavy hand creates air bubbles in the mixture, and when the air bubbles bake, the result is a rough, cratered surface on the top of the custard. It still tastes great, but it looks less than beautiful. So proceed gently.

FLOWER SORBET

What, exactly, is a sorbet? It's a frozen dessert made with sugar and fruit juice or flavored water. No dairy. And since you're now an expert at making foraged flower syrups, making a sorbet should be a piece of cake.

The prettiest sorbet I've made is with locust flowers. The addition of lemon juice turns the infusion from purple to bright magenta. You can also make delicious sorbets from pineapple weed, plum blossoms, magnolia flowers, honeysuckle flowers, and rose petals.

YIELD: APPROXIMATELY 4 CUPS

2 cups flower blossoms	2 cups water
2 cups sugar, divided	1 lemon, juice only

Remove the flowers from their stems and put them in a bowl. Add ¼ cup sugar, and, with a pestle, mash the flowers into the sugar. Keep at it, mashing and stirring, until the flowers have formed a sort of paste. My 2 cups of flowers reduced to about ½ cup of paste.

Combine the water and the remaining sugar in a saucepan and bring it to a boil, whisking to dissolve the sugar. Add the flower paste, stir, and reduce the heat to a simmer. Let the syrup simmer for 10 minutes, then remove it from the heat, cover, and let it cool for at least an hour or overnight.

Strain off the solids, pressing down on them to extract as much liquid as possible. Then strain the syrup one more time to catch any little bits and pieces that may have come through with the pressing.

Add the lemon juice. If you're using locust flowers, prepare to be amazed by the color change. The dark purple syrup turns magenta when it reacts with the acid.

Refrigerate the syrup for at least an hour, then process in your ice cream maker.

If you have a few leftover blossoms, sprinkle them on top of the sorbet when you serve it. A feast for the eyes and the stomach.

STUFFED YUCCA
FLOWERS

Yucca flowers are perfect little bite-sized packages, so why not fill them with something delicious. Start with a cream cheese base, then add your favorite flavorings. It's ok if they're not all foraged. I'll allow it.

You'll use the whole yucca flower in this recipe, but remove the pistils and stamens first. Grasp them at the base where they join the flower and give a quick twist. These flower parts cook more slowly than the flower petals, so we'll give them a head start.

YIELD: 25 STUFFED FLOWERS

25 rinsed yucca flowers, pistils and stamens removed and reserved

1/4 cup chopped onion

Olive oil

1/2 teaspoon salt

1/2 teaspoon ground sumac

2 tablespoons chopped green chiles

1/2 cup cream cheese, room temperature

All-purpose flour

1 egg, beaten

Roughly chop the yucca pistils and stamens, add to the onion, and sauté in olive oil until the onion is translucent. The pistils and stamens may (or may not) turn green. (It's a quirk of yucca blossoms.) Add the salt, sumac powder, and whichever kind of pepper you prefer and stir to combine, then remove from the heat. You don't need to cook the spices and peppers, just warm them up a little.

Place the cream cheese in a bowl and fold in the warmed ingredients to distribute them evenly.

Place a teaspoon full of the cheese mixture inside each yucca flower and gently press the flowers closed. Dip each flower in the beaten egg, then lightly dredge in flour and set aside.

In a clean sauté pan, add more olive oil and fry the stuffed blossoms until the cream cheese becomes soft and melty and the outside of each flower is a crispy golden brown. Serve warm.

NOTE: If you're not a fan of spicy food, you can substitute chopped, roasted red bell peppers for the green chiles.

CATTAIL FLOWER
BREAKFAST

Cattails flowers have such a special flavor: mild, sweet, and reminiscent of corn, but more delicate. I suggest letting the main ingredient shine. No need for lots of spices here, although if you want to add salt and pepper before you dig in, feel free!

YIELD: 2 (6-OUNCE) SERVINGS

3 eggs

1 cup male cattail flowers

$\frac{1}{2}$ cup grated Parmesan cheese

$\frac{1}{4}$ cup breadcrumbs

Preheat your oven to 350°F and generously grease two 6-ounce ramekins.

Whisk the eggs in a bowl, add the cattail flowers, cheese, and breadcrumbs, and combine thoroughly. Pour the mixture into ramekins or ovenproof dishes, stopping $\frac{1}{2}$ inch below the rim.

Bake for 15 minutes or until a knife stuck in the center of the dish comes out clean.

This simple breakfast dish is light, yet filling. It's extra special to me because the season is so short, and I know I'll only be able to enjoy it once or twice a year.

Raw nettles and Nettle Malfatti (page 99)

GREENS

Greens are the mainstay of the forager's pantry. They're easy to harvest in quantity, nutritious, versatile, and simple to preserve. They offer a wide range of flavors and textures: tart, earthy, bitter, mild, crunchy, soft, succulent. If my freezer isn't full of neat little vacuum-sealed packages of wild greens, well, then that isn't my freezer.

There are millions things you can do with wild greens, and the more you play with them, the more you'll appreciate them. I categorize greens in a few different ways. There are leafy greens and there are shoots (young stems, like asparagus). There are greens that are best eaten raw, and some that must only be eaten cooked. There are bitter greens, mild greens, fuzzy greens, smooth greens, and prickly greens. Naturally, you know to serve greens as vegetables, but they also make excellent cocktail ingredients, smoothies, and, yes, even desserts.

Probably the most important distinction to make when thinking about greens recipes is the bitterness quotient. Everyone has their own tolerance level for bitter flavors and that's perfectly ok. Remember, bitter isn't always bad. Some traditional vegetables like radicchio and arugula are intensely bitter, but they are delicious when prepared properly or combined with milder greens in a mixed greens dish. And if all you have are bitter greens, there are several ways to tame the flavor if it's too strong for you:

- Blanching A quick blanch works wonders for most bitter greens. Some intensely bitter greens require blanching in several changes of water.
- Strong flavors Try balancing the bitterness with strong flavors like bacon, sausage, garlic, strong cheese, or hot peppers.
- Acid Vinegar and citrus are classic ingredients that counterbalance bitterness.
- Salt Salt mellows bitterness in raw or cooked greens. And remember, the salt can come from many sources: anchovies, feta cheese, cured meats, or plain old sea salt.
- Sweetener A little maple or birch syrup, some honey, or brown sugar will balance bitterness.
- Fat Cream, butter, and cheese will all temper bitterness.
- Braising Slow cooking in liquid will soften the texture and mellow the flavor of bitter greens.
- Ice water If you're committed to eating raw greens, an ice water soak for 30 minutes will remove some (not all) of the bitterness.
- Massage Sounds weird, doesn't it? But massaging raw greens alleviates a lot of bitterness. Try experimenting with two leaves from the same dandelion plant. Rub one between your fingers until it feels wilted, then taste that and compare the flavor to an unmassaged leaf. For bitter greens you'd like to use raw, this is a good way to go.

Preserving the Harvest

Wild greens are a welcome sight, especially in the spring after a winter of preserved foods. Because you've just harvested these greens locally and they haven't been shipped thousands of miles, you'll probably be able to store them in the fridge for at least a week. If you'd like to stretch that time a little longer, wash and dry your greens, then loosely pack them in a hard-sided container lined with a paper towel. Put another paper towel on top and close the lid. Store the container in the crisper drawer, and you should be able to get 10–14 days out of them.

DEHYDRATION

Lots of people dehydrate their greens, then use the powder to thicken soups or make teas. I don't. I feel that too much flavor is lost by drying, so I can't recommend this method.

BLANCHING & FREEZING

This is by far my favorite way to preserve wild greens. Of course, you'll lose some of the texture, but this method preserves the most flavor and some of the texture of the fresh green. And thanks to Harold McGee (author of *On Food and Cooking*), I can explain why.

Freezing your greens stops their metabolic processes. When the water in plant tissue freezes, it becomes immobile, and this, in turn, immobilizes most other molecules in the plant, causing *most* chemical activity to come to a screeching halt.

Notice how I said "most?" Some chemical reactions are actually enhanced by freezing. The formation of ice crystals speeds up the enzymatic breakdown of both pigments and vitamins by concentrating the enzymes and other molecules responsible for these processes. As a result, your frozen food will thaw to be less beautiful and less nutritious than it was when it was fresh.

That's where blanching comes in. Blanching stops the enzymatic breakdown of pigments and vitamins, and the subsequent shock of an ice water bath stops the cooking. Overcook your greens and you'll be left with mush. Undercook, and your frozen greens will end up a dull color with reduced nutrients. To blanch the leafy greens in this chapter, boil them one to two minutes. Stems (like milkweed) and leaf/bud combinations (like white top mustard) will require a few more minutes.

When your greens have completely cooled, strain them and squeeze out as much water as possible to minimize the accumulation of ice crystals in the plant tissue. These sharp crystals puncture the plants' cell walls and destroy the structure of the plants, once again leaving you with mush.

If you plan to freeze your greens for more than a few weeks, use a vacuum sealer to package them with as little air as possible. Contact between cold, dry air and frozen foods can lead to freezer burn. Because water seeks equilibrium, and because the air in your freezer is very dry, ice crystals evaporate from frozen food into the air. This results in stale flavor and tough texture.

CANNING

There's only one problem with freezing greens, and that is storage. Most of us have limited freezer space, and if you live someplace where regular electric service is problematic, relying on a freezer may not be practical.

Using a pressure canner to can your greens lets you store jars of them without using electricity and leaves your freezer space available for important things like ice cream. But be aware that canning will result in even softer greens than blanching and freezing. For certain recipes, this may be a plus. For others, not so much.

PICKLING

I've said it before and I'll say it again: most pickles taste more like the brine than the original ingredient. I don't pickle many greens, but the thicker stems and leaves of purslane make a nice crunchy pickle, as do fiddleheads and Japanese knotweed shoots.

Seasonal Availability

Most greens are best harvested in cool weather (spring and fall), although there are several that flourish in summer heat. The best tip I can give you is to harvest before the plant goes to flower. The older the plant gets, the more fibrous and

	Spring	Summer	Fall	Winter
amaranth (*Amaranthus* spp.)	X	X		
chickweed (*Stellaria media*)	X		X	X
curly dock (*Rumex crispus*)	X		X	X
dandelion (*Taraxacum* spp.)	X		X	X
daylily (*Hemerocallis fulva*)	X	X		
fiddleheads (*Matteuccia struthiopteris*)	X			
garlic mustard (*Alliaria petiolata*)	X		X	
goutweed (*Aegopodium podagraria*)	X			
Japanese knotweed (*Fallopia japonica*)	X			
lamb's quarters (*Chenopodium* spp.)		X	X	
milkweed (*Asclepias* spp.)	X			
mustard greens (various species)	X			
pokeweed (*Phytolacca Americana*)	X			
purslane (*Portulaca oleracea*)		X		
sochan (*Rudbeckia laciniata*)	X		X	
stinging nettle (*Urtica dioica*)	X	X		
watercress (*Nasturtium officinale*)	X	X	X	X
wood nettle (*Laportea canadensis*)	X	X		

less tender its leaves and stems will be. Some research suggests that plants produce more bitter compounds when they are ripening seed. This makes them less tasty to predators and allows the plant to propagate itself. Generally, harvesting before a plant flowers and ripens seed will give you less bitter, less fibrous greens.

You may read that wild shoots like pokeweed, milkweed, and knotweed should only be harvested when they are six to eight inches tall. Height is not the important thing here, tenderness is. As Sam Thayer explains in *Incredible Wild Edibles*, the important thing is to harvest these shoots when they are in their meristematic stage of growth. This means that the plant's cells are dividing rapidly and the plant tissue will be at its tender best. If you can easily snap these shoots off the base of the plant with your hand, they're tender enough to harvest. If you meet resistance, try moving up the stem a few inches more to find a softer spot.

All varieties of amaranth (*Amaranthus* spp.) are considered edible, including the gorgeous, multicolored cultivars usually sold as ornamental plants. Redroot pigweed (*A. retroflexus*), Palmer's amaranth (*A. palmeri*), and *A. hybridus* are three of the most common wild amaranths. These are plants that prefer disturbed soils, so look in fields, yards, and parks. Like lamb's quarters, amaranth is a summer green that can stand the heat. It can be used as a spinach substitute and tastes better cooked than raw. Many cultures around the world appreciate amaranth greens and seeds (used as a grain), but in the United States, they are usually condemned as agricultural weeds. This is a mild green you can preserve by blanching and freezing.

Chickweed (*Stellaria media*) is a mild, cool-weather green. In some places it will stay green and harvestable all winter, but not where I live. It's an annual plant, emerging early in the year and dying back in warm weather. Depending on your climate, you may get a second round of growth when seeds germinate in fall, or they may not sprout until the following spring. Chickweed is a mild green and makes a good salad. If you want to add it to cooked greens dishes to balance a bitter green, add it at the very end of your cooking—because it is tender and delicate, it requires very little heat. The flowers are also edible.

Curly dock (*Rumex crispus*) is one of the earliest greens to emerge in spring. I love the flavor and texture of this plant, not to mention the fact that you'll often be able to harvest another round of fresh foliage in fall. Pick young leaves from the center of the plant; leaves that haven't completely unfurled are the most tender and delicious. Dock foliage is extremely mucilaginous, which makes it more enjoyable to eat cooked than raw. I use the leaves to thicken soups (see the gumbo recipe on page 42) and in egg dishes, where the dock becomes meltingly delicious. So creamy and good. Blanch and freeze dock greens for future use.

Dandelions are almost universally recognized. This is a bitter, cool-weather green, best harvested in spring, fall, or winter (if you live somewhere with a mild climate). Summer heat usually makes dandelions too bitter and tough to be tasty. Harvest the leaves before flowers emerge and taste a raw leaf to determine how you'll proceed. You may want to blanch them once to remove the bitter edge. In cool weather, raw dandelions may be palatable; in summer, multiple blanches may be required. After blanching, you can freeze dandelions to preserve for future use.

Daylily (*Hemerocallis fulva*) greens have a rich, nutty flavor. This is a mild green with a texture halfway between that of stem and leaf. This crunchy texture makes them an excellent ingredient for soups, stir-fries, and egg dishes. Harvest the young stems when they're about six inches tall. You may blanch and freeze daylily greens to preserve them, but they'll lose their crunch when thawed. Note that a small percentage of people have an allergic reaction to daylilies—if you've never eaten them before, please try a small amount the first time you eat them.

There are several species of ferns that produce edible fiddleheads, but the fiddleheads of the ostrich fern (*Matteuccia struthiopteris*) are generally considered the most delicious. Fiddleheads should be harvested in moderation. Always leave at least three on the plant to unfurl and photosynthesize. Overharvesting will weaken the plant and decrease future harvests. The FDA recommends boiling or steaming fiddleheads for at least fifteen minutes, citing a series of food poisonings emanating from a single food processing plant in Canada in 1994. Many foragers prefer to cook their fiddleheads for less time to maintain the crunch. You should decide for yourself what feels comfortable for you.

Garlic mustard (*Alliaria petiolata*) is the bane of every environmentalist's existence. It's an invasive, biennial plant that produces allelopathic compounds which inhibit germination of neighboring plants. As a result, you'll often find carpets of garlic mustard crowding out less aggressive natives. If you harvest first-year plants before they set seed and pull up the entire root, you can take the plant back to the kitchen to cook with and help tidy up your local environment at the same time. Garlic mustard leaves have a strong garlic flavor and smell like garlic when you tear into a leaf. This is a bitter green that can be eaten raw or cooked. It freezes well.

Goutweed (*Aegopodium podagraria*) is often grown as an ornamental by people who have no idea that it's also edible. The variegated variety is more popular in modern gardens, while the solid green species is often found in the wild or at old homestead sites. The flavor is reminiscent of celery, with the variegated variety being less strongly flavored. Goutweed can be used as a mild green to balance bitter greens in cooked applications, but I most enjoy it raw in salads and chimichurri sauces.

Japanese knotweed (*Fallopia japonica*) is another aggressive weed that strikes fear in the hearts of homeowners and ecologists alike. The flexible, young stems and the flexible tips of older stems make an excellent vegetable. The flavor is tart and earthy—it can take the place of rhubarb in desserts. You should be able to snap off the stem with a noticeable pop. If you don't hear that distinctive sound, the stem is too old and fibrous to be tasty. Some people enjoy knotweed stems raw, but I prefer them cooked. Knotweed does not require blanching prior to freezing, so harvest as much as you like (you will *not* make a dent in the population), and freeze it until you have time to play with your harvest.

When you harvest Japanese knotweed, you'll notice the green stems are flecked with red. This is interesting because knotweed syrup is pink, while cooked knotweed is green. They have similar flavors, but the colors are completely different.

Lamb's quarters (*Chenopodium album*) is often called wild spinach. It's a mild green that can be eaten raw or cooked, but the application of heat greatly improves the flavor and texture. This is a summer green and is often found in large quantities, making it a nice green to harvest at a time of year when many greens are too tough to be tasty. Most people eat only the leaves, but the stems can also be eaten. After stripping off the leaves, steam the stems like asparagus. Lamb's quarters should be harvested before the plant blooms. Both leaves and stems can be preserved by blanching and freezing.

There are many species of milkweed, but the two common milkweeds (*Asclepias syriaca* in the eastern United States and *A. speciosa* in the western states) are the only species I recommend as edible. You may read that milkweed is bitter and requires boiling in several changes of water, but this is not the case.

Some foragers suspect this rumor was started by someone who mistook dogbane for milkweed. (Dogbane, a close relative of milkweed, is indeed very bitter.) Milkweed's flavor is similar to that of green beans. Stems should be harvested when they're tender enough to snap off, usually when they're about 6–10 inches tall. Milkweed leaves can be bitter, so remove all but the last pair of leaves at the top of the stalk, then use the stems fresh, or blanch and freeze to preserve. All green parts of these milkweeds exude a sticky white latex when broken. A quick blanch will make this go away.

There are so many varieties of mustard greens, I cannot list them all here. Mustards are generally sharp, with a flavor similar to that of horseradish, but some are stronger than others. Musk mustard (*Chorispora tenella*) is on the mild side with mushroomy undertones. Whitetop (*Lepidium draba*) and wintercress (*Barbarea vulgaris*) are more bitter and require one or two blanches to tone down the bitterness. Despite that, white top is one of my favorite mustards. I harvest the immature floret and several leaf pairs and treat that as I would broccoli rabe. Whichever mustard grows where you forage, taste a leaf raw first. If it's too bitter to be pleasant, blanch it once and taste again. Still too bitter? Blanch it again! You can either cook with it now, freeze for future use, or swear you'll never waste your time foraging for this particular mustard green again.

Pokeweed (*Phytolacca Americana*) is sometimes called poke sallet, but I don't use this term because it misleads people into thinking it can be eaten raw, which it cannot. This is not a salad green. The raw plant is toxic; it *must* be cooked. Pokeweed should be boiled for ten minutes, then drained and tasted. If it is at all bitter, boil again for another ten minutes in a change of water. Both the young leaves and the tender shoots are edible. Remember, the tenderness of the shoot is the important thing, not the size of the shoot. If you can snap it off easily by hand, it's good to go. Harvest before the plant begins to flower. After flowers form, the stem will be too fibrous to be tasty. You may freeze blanched pokeweed to preserve for later use. This is a mild green.

Purslane (*Portulaca oleracea*) is a succulent green that thrives in summer heat. Its flavor is tart and its texture is crunchy. It's great raw in salads or cooked in stir-fries. Combined with tequila in a blender, it makes a delicious, deep green adult beverage. This is an exceptionally nutritious plant, higher in omega-3 fatty acids than most leafy greens. And because of its texture and succulence, it reduces less in volume than most greens. I prefer using purslane fresh, because freezing and thawing removes the enjoyably characteristic crunch.

Sochan (*Rudbeckia laciniata*) is inexplicably underrated, even among foragers. A common garden ornamental, it is also found in the wild, usually in riparian areas. Like daylily greens, spring sochan greens have a rich flavor: not sharp, but not bland. After flowering, the plant puts out another round of fresh greens, and these have a slightly stronger flavor, almost like bok choy. They can be cooked fresh or blanched and frozen for future use. And if you love the flavor as much as I do, you'll plant some in your garden, both for their flavor and for their lovely blooms.

Stinging nettles (*Urtica dioica*) have made their way onto some restaurant menus, but they deserve wider appreciation. While some people claim to be able to eat the leaves raw, I have no desire to risk a mouthful of pain. I've been stung other places often enough to respect the nettle's armaments. Fortunately, the stingers are easily neutralized by blanching. The flavor of stinging nettles is rich and mild. You can prepare nettles any way you'd cook spinach, and if you boil them, save the cooking liquid. It's a nutritious beverage made even better with the addition of a little lemon, ginger, and a touch of sweetener. Harvest before the plant starts to flower. After that, the stems will be unpleasantly fibrous and tough.

Watercress (*Nasturtium officinale*) is a member of the mustard family, but I'm giving it its own profile because of its unique characteristics. Watercress has a sharp, peppery flavor, and it grows in cool, slow-moving streams. As long as the water doesn't freeze, you can harvest watercress, making it a wonderful discovery for the winter forager. Eating raw watercress can be problematic if the water it grows in is polluted by animal waste. The liver fluke (a parasite) may inhabit the underwater parts of the plant, and eating this parasite has dire consequences. Fortunately, boiling watercress for a few minutes kills the parasite, so yay. Also, liver fluke that inhabits watercress is at an immobile stage, so harvesting above the waterline should be safe. You should make your own informed decision on how you'd like to eat watercress.

Wood nettles (*Laportea canadensis*) are less well known than stinging nettles, but they are equally tasty and equally well armed. This is another mild green that should be cooked before eating. Both wood nettles and stinging nettles can be blanched and frozen for future use.

Summary of Flavor Profiles	
amaranth	mild
chickweed	mild
curly dock	tart
dandelions	usually bitter
daylily	mild
fiddleheads	mild
garlic mustard	bitter, garlicky
goutweed	mild
Japanese knotweed	tart
lamb's quarters	mild
milkweed	mild
mustard greens	various, but mostly bitter
pokeweed	mild
purslane	mild
sochan	mild
stinging nettles	mild
watercress	sharp
wood nettles	mild

General Techniques

RAW

You probably know how to make a salad, so I won't go into great detail here. However, I will suggest that if you're using raw, bitter greens, start by using about 30% bitter and 70% mild greens, then adjust the balance to suit your personal taste. Bitter greens can be chopped into smaller pieces to make them less formidable in a salad, and you can always massage them to soften the bitter edge of some raw greens.

ROASTING

This technique lets the flavor of your foraged ingredient shine, and it's great for stems and shoots like milkweed and knotweed. Milkweed should be blanched first to remove the white latex. Shock the blanched greens in cold water, then let them dry. Toss them in olive oil, salt, and pepper, and roast them at 425°F for 10 minutes. A dusting of garlic powder or Parmesan cheese would not be unwelcome. Roasted knotweed is a tart vegetable and substitutes nicely for sorrel.

BRAISING

Sharp, bitter, and slightly tough greens are well-served by extended cooking in liquid, whether that be water, broth, wine, or a combination of all three—maybe with a little lemon juice or a splash of vinegar thrown in. The tougher the leaf, the longer you'll want to braise your greens. The order of business is this: wash and chop the greens, then place them in a pot and cover them with your liquid of choice. You may need to cook the greens anywhere from 5–45 minutes.

STIR-FRY

Many of the greens in this chapter, both leaves and stems, are delicious in a simple stir-fry. And by simple, I mean sautéed in olive oil with something in the *Allium* family. You might add a squeeze of lemon juice, a crumble of cheese, or a little Greek yogurt, but your goal here is to taste the foraged ingredient to get familiar with its flavor before you start adding lots of additional ingredients.

HORTOPITA

If you've ever had spinach pie (*spanakopita*), this dish may sound familiar. And if you've ever had *spanakopita* in Greece, you may actually have had *hortopita*, which is what this recipe is for. *Horta* is the Greek word for greens, and *pita* means pie. In rural Greece, you're more likely to be served a pita filled with a mix of greens than one made with spinach. It's a can't-miss recipe that uses many of the techniques described on page 88 for making the most of bitter greens, combining them with strong cheese, alliums, and herbs.

If you've never worked with phyllo dough before, you may be surprised at how easy it is. The key to success is to prevent the phyllo from drying out and getting so brittle that it breaks. Soak a clean dish towel with water, squeeze out every bit of excess water, then drape it over the rolled-out dough. The moisture in the towel will keep the dough pliable.

While my *yiayia* made her own phyllo dough, I do not. (Come on, I already told you I don't make my own pie crusts. Did you think I was going to make my own phyllo?) Most American supermarkets carry it in the freezer case. Most Greek supermarkets do, too, so that tells you something.

This recipe is for an 11 x 17-inch baking pan. You may adjust the quantities to make a larger or smaller batch, but be sure to cut the phyllo to fit the size of your pan. Try this with a 50/50 blend of mild greens (e.g. nettles, lamb's quarters, chickweed) and bitter ones (dandelions, mustard greens, or watercress).

YIELD: 1 (11 X 17-INCH) PAN

Olive oil

1 cup chopped onion

4 cups fresh foraged greens, roughly chopped (or 2 cups blanched, drained, and chopped)

1 tablespoon dry, crumbled bee balm

1 teaspoon field garlic powder

1 cup crumbled feta cheese

1 cup plain Greek yogurt

2 eggs, slightly beaten

1 teaspoon salt

$\frac{1}{2}$ teaspoon pepper

1 package commercial phyllo dough

Olive oil spray

continued

Preheat the oven to 350°F.

Heat a few tablespoons of olive oil in a large pan and cook the onion until tender and translucent. Add the greens and cook to reduce, then remove from the heat and let cool.

Once the greens are at room temperature, add the bee balm, garlic powder, feta, yogurt, and eggs, and combine thoroughly. Add the salt and pepper, then taste and adjust as needed. Set the greens mixture aside.

Open the plastic wrap surrounding the phyllo and unroll the dough. Spread the phyllo out on the counter and cut through the layers to make it fit the bottom of your baking pan. Now, cover the phyllo with a damp dishtowel, as described above.

Spray the bottom of the pan with olive oil spray and lay down a piece of phyllo. (You could use olive oil applied with a brush instead of spray oil, but with spray you'll be less likely to tear the dough.) Spray the phyllo with olive oil and place another piece on top of the first, and spray that, too. Repeat until you have 4 layers of phyllo. Don't forget, keep the unused dough covered with the damp dish towel while you're assembling the pie.

Take half of the greens mixture and spread it evenly across the phyllo. Place another 4 layers of phyllo on top of the greens, spraying between each one.

Spread the remainder of the greens on top of the top layer of phyllo, and again, add 4 layers of dough, spraying each layer with oil.

Using a sharp knife, score the top layer (or two) of the phyllo into rectangles. If you wait until after you've cooked the pita, the dough will crack when cut. Scoring the raw phyllo makes for neater cutting later on.

Bake for 45 minutes, or until the top layer of phyllo is golden brown and crispy. Check the pan halfway through and rotate if it's browning unevenly. Remove from the oven, let it cool slightly, then cut and serve.

GREENS SOUP

While you could make this soup with a blend of greens, making it with a single type of green gives you a pure flavor experience. My favorites are nettles, watercress, knotweed, and pokeweed.

YIELD: 6 CUPS

Olive oil

1/2 cup chopped onion

1/2 cup thinly sliced Jerusalem artichokes (or potatoes or cooked rice)

2 cups blanched greens, roughly chopped

1 teaspoon salt

Pepper, to taste

4 cups chicken or vegetable stock

1/2 cup yogurt, cream, or crème fraîche

Ground, dried cow parsnip seed and/or ground dried sumac

Heat a tablespoon of olive oil in a sauté pan, then add the onion and Jerusalem artichoke. Cook, stirring over medium heat, until the onion becomes translucent, but don't let brown. (Browned onions are delicious, but that is not the flavor we're going for here.)

Add the chopped and blanched greens to the onion and Jerusalem artichokes, then add the salt, pepper, and stock. Bring the ingredients to a boil, then reduce the heat and simmer for 20–30 minutes. The Jerusalem artichokes (or potatoes or rice) should be entirely soft.

Transfer the mixture to a blender and pulverize to make a smooth purée. You may have to do this in batches depending on the size of your blender. Pour the soup into a saucepan and stir in the dairy. If you have an immersion blender, use that to purée your soup in the pan. (This works best in a high-walled soup pot. Using an immersion blender in a shallow pan can be messy!)

Taste and adjust the seasoning, if necessary. Pour the soup into bowls and sprinkle with a pinch of cow parsnip seed or sumac powder, depending on the green. I like to use sumac with nettles and pokeweed, and cow parsnip seed with knotweed and watercress.

If you'd like to freeze or can your foraged greens soup to enjoy later, stop before adding the dairy, and resume there just before serving.

PESTO

The word pesto comes from the Italian word *peste*, meaning to pound. So while we're most familiar with the basil and pine nuts combination, pesto can be any sauce made from raw ingredients crushed in a mortar and pestle. Or, what the heck, in a food processor.

YIELD: APPROXIMATELY 2 CUPS

1/4 cup olive oil

1/2 teaspoon salt

1/2 teaspoon pepper

3 cloves garlic, peeled (if you have fresh field garlic, use 3 cleaned fresh bulbs)

4 cups foraged greens, roughly chopped

1/2 cup nut of choice

1/2 cup grated Parmesan or Romano cheese

1 tablespoon lemon juice

Some people insist pesto must be hand ground in a mortar and pestle. I do not.

I use either a food processor or a blender, but I'm careful to *not* create a silky-smooth sauce. I want my pesto to have a nice, toothsome grain.

Combine all of the ingredients in your blender or food processor and start the machine on its lowest setting. Watch to make sure all the big chunks run through the blades, then turn it off. Check the texture, and if you'd like a smoother sauce, go ahead and blend a little more, but hands off the high-speed button!

Pesto can be added to rice or pasta, of course. And a few tablespoons added to vegetable or chicken stock will amp up the flavor of your next soup. It's also great spread on a really good slice of toasted bread.

If you make this pesto with garlic mustard leaves, you may omit the actual garlic. Some of my favorite combinations are dandelion greens with black walnuts, nettles with toasted pumpkin seeds, and mustard greens with pine nuts. All of these freeze well for future use.

GREENS & GRAINS
CASEROLE

This is another recipe that accommodates a wide range of greens. You can make it as sharp or as mild as you like. If you only have bitter greens, increase the cheese by 50% to balance the flavors.

This is a great way to use up leftover grains: brown rice, wild rice, quinoa, farro, bulgur, and freekeh all work well.

YIELD: 1 (9 X 9-INCH) CASSEROLE OR 8 TO 10 INDIVIDUAL SERVINGS

1 cup cooked grains

1 cup chopped wild greens, blanched and drained (if you're using frozen/thawed greens, squeeze out as much water as possible before using them)

1½ tablespoons field garlic powder

½ tablespoon bee balm powder

1 cup grated Romano or Parmesan cheese (1½ cups if you're working with only bitter greens)

2 eggs

¼ cup sour cream or plain yogurt

1 teaspoon salt

¼ teaspoon pepper

1 tablespoon butter, cut into pieces

Preheat the oven to 350°F.

Combine the first 5 ingredients in a large bowl and mix together well.

In a separate bowl, whisk together the eggs, sour cream, salt, and pepper, then add this to the greens and grains mixture and combine well.

This dish can be made as a single large casserole or as individual servings in a muffin tin. Whichever you choose, grease the cooking vessel and fill it with the mixture. Press the mixture firmly into the dish. You want it to be 1–1½ inches deep, so choose your dish accordingly. Keeping the casserole thin guarantees the best ratio of crispy, golden crust to chewy filling.

Dot the top of the casserole with butter and bake for 30–40 minutes until the casserole is set and golden brown at the edges. Standard-sized muffins should bake for 25 minutes.

Serve this dish warm or at room temperature.

NOTE: If bee balm isn't your favorite flavor, there are lots of other wild spices that work well in this recipe. You could substitute:

1 tablespoon mushroom powder	umami
1 tablespoon ground sumac	tartness
½ teaspoon juniper berry powder	herbal, citrusy bitterness
½ teaspoon pink peppercorns (ground)	spicy heat (leave out the black pepper)

Just don't use them all at once!

GREENS SOUFFLÉ

For years, just thinking about the word "soufflé" made me nervous. When I finally got up the nerve to give it a try, I wondered what took me so long. Follow the instructions with precision and you'll have no trouble creating a light, fluffy, foraged greens soufflé.

All of the leafy greens in this chapter work well in this recipe. I like a combination of mild and sharp greens, but feel free to choose according to your personal taste. This recipe works equally well with fresh or frozen greens. Blanch or steam the greens until they are soft, squeeze out as much liquid as possible from the greens after cooking, then purée them in a food processor.

YIELD: 1 SOUFFLÉ OR 4 SMALL SOUFFLÉS

$1^{1}/_{2}$ cups milk (nut milks work fine)

4 tablespoons butter, plus more for buttering the soufflé dishes

$^{1}/_{4}$ cup all-purpose flour

6 eggs, separated

$^{1}/_{2}$ teaspoon salt

$^{1}/_{2}$ teaspoon pepper

1 teaspoon ground mustard

$^{1}/_{4}$ teaspoon cayenne

2 tablespoons minced onion

1 cup puréed wild greens

$^{1}/_{2}$ cup grated or crumbled cheese (Parmesan, Swiss, cheddar, and feta all work well)

Preheat your oven to 375°F.

Warm the milk in the microwave for about 1 minute at full power. Remove from the microwave and set this aside. If you prefer to warm your milk in a saucepan, warm it until the milk just begins to steam; do not simmer or boil.

In a small saucepan, melt 4 tablespoons of butter over medium heat. Add the flour and whisk together until the mixture darkens slightly. (This will take 3–4 minutes.) Reduce the heat to low and gradually add the warmed milk, whisking to combine smoothly. Continue to whisk over low heat until the mixture thickens enough to coat the back of a spoon.

Remove the mixture from the heat and let it cool for several minutes. Then add the egg yolks, one at a time, whisking each one into the milk mixture. Add the salt, pepper, ground mustard, cayenne, onion, puréed wild greens, and cheese. Transfer the mixture to a bowl and set aside.

You may make this recipe as a single, larger soufflé or in 4 (1-cup) soufflé dishes. Use the extra butter to grease the soufflé dish(es). Solid butter works better than butter spray in this instance because it stays in place on the soufflé dish; sprays tend to run down the sides.

In a clean bowl, use an electric mixer to whip the egg whites to soft peaks. Add ⅓ of the whipped egg whites to the greens mixture and stir it together well. Then add the remainder of the egg whites and fold them into the batter slowly and gently.

Pour the batter into the buttered soufflé dishes to within about ½ inch of the edge of the dish.

Transfer the filled dishes to a baking sheet and put the sheet on the lowest rack of the preheated oven. Placing the soufflés as close as possible to the heat (which comes from the bottom of the oven) will help you get a good rise.

Set your timer for 15 minutes for small soufflé dishes or 30 minutes for a single, larger soufflé. When the time is up, if the soufflés have risen and the tops look golden brown, check for doneness with a toothpick or cake tester. The interiors should be moist, not wet, and the tester should come out clean. You may need an additional 5 minutes, but don't overcook.

Once your soufflés are done, serve them immediately; they'll start to fall as soon as they begin to cool. Soufflés can be reheated and will rise again, although not to their original height. Vegetable-based soufflés like this one don't rise as dramatically as a plain soufflé, but they also don't fall as much when they cool.

This foraged greens soufflé makes a superb breakfast, an excellent vegetarian lunch, or an elegant side dish at dinner.

NETTLE MALFATTI

Malfatti is Italian for "poorly made," which does not do justice to the dish. Lighter than *gnocchi* or *gnudi*, *malfatti* are made from the kinds of leftovers you might find in any country kitchen: breadcrumbs, eggs, a bit of cheese. And if you don't have nettles growing outside, substitute another mild green, like lamb's quarters or amaranth. This recipe calls for four ounces of raw nettles, but you can scale it up or down to fit your harvest.

YIELD: 2 TO 3 DOZEN

4 ounces raw nettles	2 eggs
1 small onion	1/2 cup grated Parmesan cheese
Olive oil	3/4 cup breadcrumbs
1 teaspoon salt	All-purpose flour
1/3 teaspoon pepper	

Prepare the nettles for cooking. Remember that raw nettles have stingers and should be handled with care. Use tongs or leather gloves to deposit your nettles in the boiling water and give them a quick blanch. Boiling for 2–3 minutes will disarm the stingers (see page 86) and turn your nettles bright green. Drain the nettles and shock them in cold water to stop the cooking. At this point, the nettles can no longer sting you, so squeeze them to release excess moisture.

Finely dice the onion and sauté it in olive oil until tender. Coarsely chop the nettles, add them to the cooked onion along with the salt and pepper, and stir to combine. Cook the mixture for 3–4 minutes, then remove it from the heat and let it cool to room temperature.

Use a food processor to finely chop the cooled nettle and onion mixture, adding more salt and pepper to taste, if necessary. Transfer the mixture to a bowl and whisk in the eggs. Next, add the Parmesan cheese and breadcrumbs and mix it all together by hand. Refrigerate and let cool for 6–8 hours. The dough becomes much easier to handle when allowed to chill.

Spread flour on a cutting board or countertop to prevent sticking. Next, flour your hands, pinch off about a tablespoon of dough, and roll it into a torpedo shape on the cutting board. Place the rolled dough on a floured baking sheet. Repeat until you have molded all your dough into torpedo shapes.

Nettle malfatti can be frozen or cooked right away for 4–5 minutes in boiling water. Serve them with brown butter, lemon zest, and a little more Parmesan cheese. A bit of crispy bacon takes this dish over the top.

COLCANNON

Traditional colcannon is an Irish dish made with potatoes and cabbage or kale. For this foraged version you may use potatoes, Jerusalem artichokes, or daylily tubers (see the Tubers and Roots chapter on page 173). Any tuber that makes a good mash makes a good colcannon; the excellent flavor and texture of the sharp greens contrast nicely with the creamy mashed potatoes.

YIELD: APPROXIMATELY 4 CUPS

$1^1/_2$ pounds tubers, chopped into 1 to 2-inch cubes

3 tablespoons butter, divided

3 cups foraged greens, finely chopped

2 tablespoons minced field garlic

$^1/_2$ cup buttermilk (cream and milk are also fine, but I like the tang of buttermilk)

Salt and pepper, to taste

Boil the potatoes, Jerusalem artichokes, or daylily tubers in salted water until tender. Drain the tubers and finely mash by passing the potatoes through a food mill or a potato ricer into a bowl.

In the potato pot, melt 2 tablespoons of butter over medium heat and add the greens and garlic. Stir and cook until the greens have wilted, then add the buttermilk and bring the mixture to a simmer.

Remove the greens from the heat and add the mashed potatoes. Combine the greens and potatoes thoroughly, add salt and pepper to taste, and serve warm with a pat of butter in the middle of each dish.

NOTE: Should you have leftovers, colcannon makes excellent pancakes. In fact, I often skip serving it as a mash and go straight to frying up colcannon cakes. A crispy, golden brown crust makes these leftovers irresistible.

Oil a griddle or frying pan and heat to medium hot.

Form the colcannon into patties about ¾ inch thick and place them on the griddle. Resist the temptation to flip them too soon. You want them to get brown and crispy on both sides.

Serve these pancakes with a little butter.

GREENS GRATIN

A gratin is a dish with a lightly browned crust of breadcrumbs or melted cheese. I like to use both! It's important to keep the layer of greens at about one inch thick to get the right proportion of greens to cheese. This recipe can be made with any combination of bitter and mild greens.

YIELD: 1 (9 X 9-INCH) PAN

1 large onion

Olive oil

6 cups greens, washed, blanched, drained, and chopped

1 teaspoon pepper

1 teaspoon salt

1 teaspoon ground spicebush berries

1 cup heavy cream

1½ cups grated Swiss or Gruyère cheese, divided

½ cup breadcrumbs

Preheat the oven to 350°F.

Roughly chop the onion, then sauté it in olive oil over medium heat until translucent. Add the greens and mix well with the onion. Incorporate the black pepper, salt, and ground spicebush berries, then remove the pan from the heat and mix in cream and 1 cup cheese. Stir well.

Transfer the mixture to a shallow, greased baking pan and, using a rubber spatula, press down on the greens to spread them out evenly. I use a 9 x 9-inch square pan, but anything with a similar area will work. The important thing is that the greens should be about 1 inch thick to give you the right greens to topping ratio.

Bake for 30 minutes, then remove the dish from the oven and sprinkle on the remaining cheese, then the breadcrumbs. Change the oven from bake to broil, then broil until the topping is golden brown. This may take 2–5 minutes, depending on your broiler and how far your pan is from the heating element. Watch carefully . . . it would be a pity to burn your spring greens gratin.

PUFF PASTRY SWIRLS

Will I sound like a broken record if I tell you I don't make my own puff pastry? Pepperidge Farm does an excellent job, and I always keep a few packages frozen for when I get the urge to make these swirls. The fluffy, crispy, buttery texture of puff pastry offers the perfect counterpoint to creamy, rich wild greens. You may use any combination you like in this recipe. The alliums and cheese help tame the bitterness of any sharp greens you may use.

YIELD: 12 TO 15 SWIRLS

½ cup roughly chopped onion or shallot

1 tablespoon olive oil

1 cup cooked wild greens, chopped, and squeezed to remove as much water as possible

¼ teaspoon field garlic powder

¾ cup cheese of choice (for bitter greens, use a strongly flavored cheese)

1 egg

1 tablespoon water

A small handful of all-purpose flour (for dusting)

1 sheet puff pastry, thawed

Preheat the oven to 400°F.

Sauté the onion in olive oil until it is soft and translucent. Add the greens and garlic powder and stir over low heat to combine. Remove from the heat and transfer to a bowl, allowing the greens mixture to cool slightly.

Add the cheese to the greens mixture and thoroughly combine. Set the bowl aside.

Beat the egg and water with a fork in a small bowl.

Spread the flour on your work surface and unfold the puff pastry sheet on top of the flour. This will prevent the pastry dough from sticking. Gently roll the dough a few times, both left to right and top to bottom, to smooth out the dough. Frozen puff pastry may crack along the fold lines and a gentle rolling will put the pieces back together. Brush the top of the sheet with the egg wash, then spread the cheese and greens mixture evenly over the puff pastry, pressing it down gently. Leave a border of about 1 inch on all four sides of the puff pastry.

Roll the puff pastry dough like a jelly roll. If the pastry sheet is rectangular, start at one of the short ends. If it's square, start from any side.

Using a serrated knife, cut the roll into ½-inch slices and lay them flat on a baking sheet (you'll probably need two). A serrated blade will cut through the thawed pastry dough much more easily than a smooth blade. Work slowly.

These swirls don't expand a lot with baking, so you can place each slice within 1 inch of the next. Use the remainder of the egg wash to brush the tops of the slices, then bake for 15 minutes or until the pastry edges are golden brown.

Remove the swirls from the baking sheet and let them cool on a rack or platter. Serve while still warm.

CURRIED GREENS
FRITTERS

Curried greens are a staple in many cuisines, and with good reason. This dish is so simple and so delicious, I often stand at the stove and eat it straight from the pan. This recipe is a great way to use bitter greens; their strong flavors work wonderfully with the curry and coconut cream.

YIELD: 12 FRITTERS

Olive oil

½ onion, roughly chopped

½ teaspoon salt

½ teaspoon pepper

2 tablespoons curry powder

2 cups blanched, chopped foraged greens

1 (13.5-ounce) can coconut cream

½ cup unflavored breadcrumbs

1 egg, beaten

Frying oil

Pour a few tablespoons of olive oil into a sauté pan and turn the heat on medium high. Sauté the onions until they are translucent, then add the salt, pepper, curry powder, and the greens. Add the coconut cream, reduce the heat and simmer for 5–10 minutes until the coconut cream is smooth and silky and the greens mixture has the texture of a *very* thick soup. Remove the greens from the heat. (This is the point where I usually sneak a taste. You could stop right here and have a very tasty side dish to serve.)

When the greens have cooled to room temperature, stir in the breadcrumbs and the egg.

Pour 1 inch of your preferred frying oil into a frying pan and use an ice cream scoop to drop scoops of batter into the hot oil. Don't crowd the pan (I do 4 at a time). Flip the fritters when the first side is golden brown.

You'll notice that the first batch of fritters takes about 3 minutes per side, the second only 2 minutes per side, and only 1–1½ per side by the third batch.

Transfer the finished fritters to a paper towel to absorb excess oil. Eat when warm! Reheat leftover fritters the next morning and eat them with a fried egg.

GREENS WONTONS

Packaged wonton wrappers simplify this recipe and provide the perfect ratio of pasta to filling. And before you ask, we've been through this before, haven't we? Wonton wrappers are in the same category (for me) as pie crusts and puff pastry. You'll find them in the produce section of your grocery store, near the tofu.

YIELD: 18 WONTONS

Olive oil

2 cloves garlic (or 2 cleaned field garlic bulbs), minced

1/2 medium onion, finely chopped

4 tablespoons fresh ginger, minced

1 tablespoon prickly ash powder

2 cups foraged greens, blanched and roughly chopped

1 tablespoon soy sauce

2 tablespoons rice wine vinegar

1 1/2 tablespoons maple syrup

Hot sauce (optional)

1 tablespoon toasted sesame seed oil

18 wonton wrappers

A small dish of water

Heat a few tablespoons of olive oil in a sauté pan, add the garlic and onion and cook over medium heat until translucent. Add the ginger and prickly ash powder and stir to combine. Add a little more olive oil to make it possible to stir, if needed.

Add the greens, soy sauce, vinegar, and maple syrup and continue to stir. Taste the greens and adjust the seasoning if needed. This is where you'll add a little hot sauce if you're a fan of spicy foods. The amount will depend on how spicy you like your food and how hot your hot sauce is. Start with 1/8 teaspoon and add more as desired.

Add sesame seed oil, stir, and remove the greens from the heat. Let the mixture cool enough that it's not difficult to handle with your bare hands.

Place a teaspoon of greens in the center of a wonton wrapper, then brush the edges of the wrapper with water and pinch the corners together at the top to form a pyramid. Press together the sides of the wrapper, using water as necessary to seal.

If you're going to fry the wontons, let air dry for 1 hour, then fry in your choice of oil until golden. If you're going to steam them, keep covered with a damp dish towel while you assemble them, then steam for about 10 minutes.

Serve with your favorite dipping sauce.

KNOTWEED CUPCAKES

This recipe can be doubled (or tripled or quadrupled) depending on how many mouths you have to feed. Before you make the cupcakes, you'll need to make a knotweed purée and a knotweed syrup. Extra purée and syrup can either be frozen or canned. The syrup should be canned in a boiling water bath for 10 minutes, and the purée should be canned in a pressure canner (15 minutes for pint or quart jars). I realize this may sound like a lot of work, but the cupcakes are delicious, and if you can some extra purée and syrup, making the cupcakes will be a lot faster and easier next time.

YIELD: 6 CUPCAKES

FOR THE PURÉE
4 cups tender Japanese knotweed stems, cut into 1-inch pieces

1 cup sugar

Water

FOR THE SYRUP
4 cups tender Japanese knotweed stems, cut into 1-inch pieces

Water

Sugar

FOR THE CUPCAKES
2 tablespoons butter, softened

½ cup sugar

6 tablespoons knotweed purée

2 tablespoons buttermilk

1 egg

½ teaspoon vanilla extract

¾ cup all-purpose flour

½ teaspoon baking powder

A pinch of salt

FOR THE FROSTING
1 egg white

¼ cup knotweed syrup

A pinch of kosher salt

To make the purée, combine the knotweed and sugar in a large pot and pour in enough water to barely cover the solids. Cook the knotweed over medium heat until the stems are soft and mushy, adding more water if necessary. This will take 15–20 minutes, and most of the water will have been absorbed or evaporated by the time the knotweed is soft enough. Add more water to extend the cooking time if necessary.

Transfer the knotweed to a blender and pulverize to make a very smooth purée.

continued

To make the syrup, place the chopped stems in a saucepan and add just enough water to cover. Bring the water to a boil, then reduce the heat and let simmer for 5 minutes, mashing occasionally to release the juices.

Pour the softened stems into a jelly bag set over a bowl and let it hang until all the juice has been extracted.

Measure the juice and return it to your saucepan. Add an equal amount of sugar and whisk the juice and sugar together over medium heat until the sugar is fully dissolved. It should feel smooth when you rub a little liquid between your fingers.

Preheat your oven to 350°F and either grease your cupcake tin or place a cupcake liner in each cup.

To make the cupcakes, use a stand mixer to thoroughly cream the butter and sugar until the color is very pale and the texture is even. Beat in the purée, buttermilk, egg, and vanilla.

In a separate bowl, combine the flour, baking powder, and salt, then add this to the wet ingredients and mix, just to combine.

Distribute the batter evenly among the prepared cups and bake for 20 minutes or until a toothpick inserted into the middle of a cupcake comes out clean. Let them cool for 5–10 minutes, then remove them from the tin and allow them to cool completely before frosting.

To make the frosting, bring water in the bottom pan of a double boiler to a rolling boil, then reduce the heat to sustain a gentle boil.

In the top of the double boiler, combine the egg white, salt, and knotweed syrup. Use an electric beater to beat the mixture constantly for 7 minutes. The texture will be quite thick and easy to spread.

Frost the cupcakes and serve at room temperature.

MUSTARD GREENS
VODKA

Mustard greens infused in vodka give the spirit a horseradish flavor that will take your martinis, Bloody Marys, and salty dog cocktails to a whole new level. You can use any mustard green in this infusion, but be aware that the stronger the mustard, the stronger your infusion.

The amounts in this recipe are for garlic mustard leaves. If it turns out stronger than you like, dilute it with uninfused vodka to get it to your perfect strength. You can also produce a lighter flavor by using half the amount of mustard leaves, by using a mustard with a lighter flavor (like musk mustard), or by letting your infusion sit for 12 hours rather than 24.

YIELD: 750 MILLILITERS

2 cups cleaned, fresh mustard leaves, roughly chopped

1 (750-milliliter) bottle vodka

Combine the mustard leaves and the vodka in a blender and pulverize to make a slurry. Transfer the mixture to a closed container and refrigerate for 24 hours.

Strain the liquid and throw away the solids. Cover and refrigerate the liquid again for 24 hours. This will allow the fine sediment to settle to the bottom of the container. Filter the liquid through a coffee filter to remove the fine sediment and transfer to a glass jar with a tight-fitting lid. Keep this in the freezer, ever at the ready to delight and amuse your guests.

Summer Pudding (page 138)

FRUIT

· ·

Fruit is seductive—just ask Eve. Who can walk past a juicy blueberry, a soft persimmon, or a cluster of perfectly ripe elderberries without being tempted to taste?

Fruit is also a gateway wild food for people who have never considered themselves foragers. I've had so many people say, "I used to love picking blackberries with my grandmother, but I never knew I was foraging!" You were, and good for you! If the promise of delicious, free fruit is all it takes to get you to become a forager then we are on the right track.

There are so many wild fruits that never make it to the grocery store or the farmers' market. Some are from plants we grow as ornamentals, never thinking to taste them. Some are so delicate and soft that they can't be shipped long distances. Others are wild or feral versions of familiar fruits you can find in cultivation.

There are also wild fruits you might not think of as fruits. Botanically speaking, a fruit is a mature ovary, which means that many things we consider vegetables are actually fruits, like milkweed pods, rose hips, and mallow cheeses.

One of the nicest things about foraged fruit is that you harvest it at its peak. Which means you get all of the flavor and none of the disappointment of biting into an unsweet watermelon or a mealy, flavorless apple. But fruit picked at its peak doesn't have a long shelf life—you'll have to use it or preserve it ASAP.

If you're going to use your fruit fresh, great! You should be able to refrigerate it for a few days without any degradation in quality. Brambleberries are the most delicate wild fruits we'll be discussing, and they should be used within one to two days, if possible. Additionally, don't wash your berries until just before you're ready to eat them. Premature washing makes your harvest mushy.

Many of us are used to letting fruit ripen on the windowsill to fully develop its flavor. This probably won't be necessary with foraged fruit, since you're harvesting at its peak, but lest you think you can harvest your wild fruit early (perhaps to beat the animals to the harvest), think again. Some people swear you can harvest mayapples when they're showing just a touch of yellow, then let them ripen indoors, but I disagree; for me, the flavor simply never develops. Some foragers harvest their serviceberries when the fruit is red, claiming that otherwise the birds take them all. I'm sure that's true, but once you've tasted a tree-ripened, dark blue serviceberry, you'll leave the red fruit for the birds. Other wild fruits—like aronia, persimmon, silverberry, and wild plums—will never lose their astringency if picked before they are fully ripe.

Preserving the Harvest

FREEZING

Preserving fruit is easy—you have multiple options. Perhaps the most familiar is freezing, which is not only simple, it makes the fruit easier to work with in some cases when it's time to get creative. Wash whole fruit first, then spread it out on a baking sheet to dry. It doesn't have to be bone dry, but you'll get fewer ice crystals if you don't pop wet fruit into the freezer. Small berries—like brambles, blueberries, mulberries, and gooseberries—can be frozen on a baking sheet for 30 to 60 minutes, then bagged in useful quantities.

You may also freeze your fruit with sugar or with syrup, depending on how you anticipate using it in the kitchen. I almost never do this because, really, who knows in June how they'll want to use their harvest in September? I don't! Most Coop Extension offices suggest that freezing fruit with sugar or syrup better preserves its color, texture, and flavor. I've never done a side-by-side comparison, and I don't plan to. But if you know you're going to make a wild strawberry pie for your husband's birthday in November, feel free to hull and sweeten the fruit before you freeze it.

Stone fruits like apricots, peaches, and plums can be frozen whole or peeled and pitted. Personally, I freeze them whole, because the skin of a thawed apricot slips right off (no parboiling required) and the pit comes out equally easily. (I'm all about saving time and labor, in case you haven't guessed by now.) The shape and texture of frozen and thawed stone fruits will be flat and soft, so this method is best for making jams, jellies, syrups, purées, and sauces.

Freezing your harvest also breaks down the cell structure of the fruit, giving you a very soft product when thawed. Softened fruit releases its flavors more quickly than fresh, solid fruit, making it ideal for infusing spirits or similar uses. It's also easier to run thawed fruit through a food mill if you're making jams or fruit butters.

If you plan to use fruit fresh but run out of time in the middle of a project, you can freeze partially processed fruit. Purées and juices can be frozen as is, and if you're lucky enough to come across an abandoned orchard of feral apples, those can be sliced and frozen to use later.

I prefer plastic containers with tightly fitting lids or vacuum-sealed bags to resealable plastic bags. These thicker, higher quality containers protect your foraged harvest from freezer burn better than thin plastic bags.

DEHYDRATION

If you don't have a dehydrator (check Craigslist—there are deals out there!), you can dry your fruit harvest using an oven or the air. Air drying will be more or less successful depending on the humidity where you live. In New Mexico, air drying is a snap, and I can dry apricot halves in less than 12 hours. In Pennsylvania, I may have to leave those same apricot halves out for two days. However long your harvest takes to dry, you'll get the best results in full sun. Lay out your fruit in a single layer on top of a screen, with another screen on top of the fruit. The two layers of screening protect the fruit from hungry animals and some insects, and let the air circulate around the fruit. Be sure to bring your setup indoors if it's going to rain—or if you have a large (and surprisingly agile) raccoon population in the neighborhood.

Oven drying is less than ideal, simply because most ovens can't be set to 135°F, which is generally recommended as the best temperature for drying fruit. The warm setting on my oven is 170°F, which is about average. If I *have* to dry something in the oven, I'll set it to 170°F and prop the door open a crack with a wooden spoon. I don't love doing this because I'm aware of wasting energy, but it's an option.

How do you know when the thing you are drying is dry enough? That depends on the thing you are drying. Herbs and spices should be crispy, while fruit is best when it's bendy. Aim for the consistency of a raisin and you'll be in good shape. I can't tell you how long you'll need to use your dehydrator, oven, or drying screens—it depends on the humidity and temperature where you live.

If you've decided to make the leap and buy a dehydrator, consider which features you really need. For me, those are a timer and a thermostat. Many inexpensive dehydrators offer neither, although it's fairly easy to set up your own timer between the outlet and the appliance. I wouldn't recommend a dehydrator without a thermostat. Different things dry best at different temperatures (for example, herbs are best dried at 95°F (see page 17), while fruit is best dried at 135°F). After going to all the trouble of gathering a substantial wild harvest, why risk losing quality by drying it at the wrong temperature?

CANNING

Canning may seem complicated (and pressure canning requires some specialized equipment), but many fruits can be canned in a boiling water bath, which can be done in a large stockpot. The benefits of canning include easy storage (no running out of freezer space) and easy access (you won't have to wait for your fruit to thaw). Plus, no one can adequately describe the satisfaction of standing in your pantry, looking at shelves full of gorgeous, foraged, home-canned fruit.

As with freezing, fruit may be canned with or without sugar. You may pressure can fruit in plain water, but if you're using a boiling water bath instead of a pressure canner, the liquid must be sweet, tart, or both. Fruit in plain water has neither enough sugar nor enough acidity to be safely canned in a boiling water bath. You may also process purées and compotes in a boiling water bath, as well as the sauces, chutneys, and jams you make from them.

General Techniques

JUICING

There are multiple ways to juice fruit. You can use a hand or a mechanical juicer, a steam juicer, or a sauté pan. I used the sauté pan for years before I purchased a steam juicer, which now I couldn't do without. Well, I could. But I don't want to. How you juice your fruit will depend on the fruit's size and texture.

Most fruits are soft enough to juice without any special equipment. Rose hips should be broken up with a few pulses in a blender or food processor—not to create a purée, but to make it easier to coax out the juices. Large fruits should be roughly chopped for the same reason.

Place the fruit in a sauté pan, barely cover with water, and bring to a boil. Reduce the heat to a slow simmer and cook until the fruit is soft enough to easily crush with a potato masher. Remove the fruit from the heat and pour it through a jelly bag or several layers of cheese cloth. Resist temptation to squeeze the bag. Squeezing the fruit may give you cloudy juice—if your endgame is a jewel-toned, crystal-clear jelly to enter in the county fair, you do *not* want cloudy juice.

A steam juicer lets you process larger quantities of fruit with less standing-by-the-stove time than a simple sauté pan. It has three parts. The bottom is a solid pan that holds water. The middle is a pan that resembles a Bundt pan with a cutout in the middle. This section has an outlet attached to a piece of translucent tubing. The top section is perforated on the sides and bottom. Most models have glass lids, which allow you to watch the progress of your fruit; some less expensive models have a metal lid.

The beauty of a steam juicer is that the steam does all the work. Fill the bottom pan with water, place the empty middle pan on top of that, then place the top pan on the middle pan and fill it with fruit. Put on the lid, turn on the heat, and wait for the magic to happen. As steam rises up through the center hole of the middle pan and the perforations of the top pan, it breaks open the skins of the fruit and the juice drips down through the perforations into the middle pan. (Note: the top pan is not perforated directly above the hole of the middle pan. This keeps the juice from dripping down into the water.) As juice collects in the second pan, you'll see it fill the tubing. Squeeze the metal clasp that keeps the tubing closed to release the juice into a container.

It takes about three hours to juice a large pan of fruit. It's not fast, but it saves you the trouble of cooking fruit in batches, transferring each batch to a jelly bag, and waiting for the juice to strain. With a steam juicer, you can check in every 30 minutes or so to collect the juice and make sure all the water hasn't boiled away.

Fruit juice can be enjoyed fresh, frozen, or canned for later. It makes a vibrant base for sorbet, ice cream, or gelatin desserts, like a light and fluffy fruit mousse (page 129). Juicing fruit is also the first step for jelly or syrup.

Once I've finished juicing (either in a steam juicer or in a sauté pan), I often run the leftover pulp through a food mill to remove any seeds. Then I sweeten the pulp just a little and make fruit leather. The best tool for this is a dehydrator, although an oven on the lowest temperature will also do the job.

Dehydrating works well for crabapples, chokecherries, plums, grapes, prickly pears, and likely many other fruits I haven't tried yet.

PURÉE

If you'd rather work with soft chunks of fruit than silky juice, turn your harvest into a fruit purée. Purées are the foundation for jams, fruit leathers, or fruit butters, and can even be substituted for butter or oil in cake recipes (page 162).

Some fruits are soft enough to purée raw, like serviceberries, perfectly ripe pawpaws, mayapples, and persimmons. Others are soft enough after being frozen and thawed. Most fruits, however, need to be heated to soften them enough for a purée. I recommend doing this by adding just enough water to keep the fruit from scorching, then simmering it until it's easy to mash. Don't add sugar at this point.

The next step is running the fruit through a food mill to give you a smooth, evenly textured purée. Most food mills come with multiple plate sizes, so you can choose one that's the right size to catch the seeds of your fruit.

ALCOHOL

Infusing fruit in alcohol takes an ordinary spirit and turns it into something extraordinary. The alcohol preserves the fruit, the fruit juice complements the flavor of the spirit, and you get the bonus of infused fruit as a leftover, which can be turned into a boozy jam, chutney, or dessert. Different fruits lend themselves to different spirits. Some of my favorite combinations include apricots infused in bourbon, blueberries with rum and a little maple syrup, and a choke-cherry bounce[1] made with rye whiskey.

For a strong fruity flavor, fill a mason jar with fruit, then add alcohol. Fill the jar with fruit halfway and top it off with alcohol for a more spirit-forward beverage. Once you've strained off the fruit, taste the liquid and decide how much sweetener you'd like. Liquid sweeteners work best in alcohol, so consider a syrup (maple, birch, shagbark hickory, or a plain simple syrup) and start by adding just a little at a time until you reach your perfect sweetness level.

Alcohol fruit infusions mellow with time, and most are best when allowed to sit for three months before straining the liquid off the solids. Bottle your booze in something pretty and astonish your friends and family with a unique adult beverage during the holidays. These infused spirits don't require refrigeration; the alcohol acts as a preservative.

VINEGAR

In the days before refrigeration, fruit was often preserved in vinegar or a combination of vinegar and sugar. Vinegar is acidic enough to make fruit inhospitable to the growth of fungi and bacteria, and sugar acts as a preservative. These concoctions are known as shrubs, or drinking vinegars, and they can be mixed with seltzer, water, or spirits to produce sweet-tart beverages (see page 55).

Seasonal Availability

The **blueberry** (*Vaccinium* spp.) is such a familiar fruit that I considered not mentioning it here. But it is also a supremely delicious fruit and the first plant many people forage for, so I couldn't leave it out. Wild blueberries are considerably smaller than their cultivated cousins, but they are packed with so much flavor that I can't bring myself to buy blueberries anymore. Low bush and high bush blueberries are equally tasty, although high bush berries are considerably easier to harvest (at least for those of us who don't love bending over for hours at a time). Blueberries can be dried, canned, or frozen. They are—it goes without

---

1. A bounce is an old-timey alcoholic beverage made with fruit and your choice of spirits, such as brandy rum, vodka, or whiskey.

	Spring	Summer	Fall	Winter
blueberries (*Vaccinium* spp.)		X		
brambleberries (*Rubus* spp.)	X	X		
chokeberries (*Aronia melanocarpa*)		X	X	
chokecherries (*Prunus virginiana*)		X		
cornelian cherries (*Cornus mas*)			X	
crabapples (*Malus* spp.)		X	X	
elderberries (*Sambucus* spp.)		X		
gooseberries (*Ribes uva-crispa*)		X		
mulberries (*Morus* spp.)	X	X		
Oregon grapes (*Mahonia* spp.)		X	X	
pawpaws (*Asimina triloba*)			X	
persimmons (*Diospyros virginiana*)			X	
plums (*Prunus* spp.)		X	X	
prickly pears (*Opuntia* spp.)		X	X	
rose hips (*Rosa* spp.)		X	X	
serviceberries or juneberries (*Amelanchier* spp.)	X			
silverberries or autumn olives (*Elaeagnus umbellata*)			X	

saying—delicious fresh off the shrub. I spent hours at summer camp picking wild blueberries, never dreaming I was a forager. This is an excellent gateway fruit.

Brambleberries (*Rubus* spp.) include familiar blackberries and raspberries, less familiar black raspberries and wineberries, and regional delicacies like dewberries, thimbleberries, and cloudberries. These are delicate fruits, with varying degrees of seediness and varying levels of armament. The long, sharp, recurved thorns of blackberries refuse to let go of the flesh, while wineberries' thin thorns are almost hairlike and easy to ignore. Brambleberries won't last long at room temperature, so refrigerate to hold them for a few days. Frozen and thawed berries taste fine but lose their shape, so this is a fruit I prefer to use fresh unless I'm using it for juice.

Chokeberries (*Aronia melanocarpa*) are not the same as chokecherries! Chokeberries are an overlooked fruit, though there has been some recent commercial interest in their high antioxidant levels. The fruit is tart (tart enough to make you choke?) and ripens in late summer to early fall. Be sure to taste a few fruits before you harvest—the fruit looks ripe (purple/black) long before it is, and unripe fruit can be astringent, while ripe fruit is merely sour. Chokeberries are often planted as ornamentals for their brilliant fall foliage. When the leaves turn bright red, the fruit is probably ripe, so get out there and start tasting. Recipes using chokeberries will need more sugar than those same recipes made with sweeter fruits. Chokeberries can be frozen to preserve.

Chokecherries (*Prunus virginiana*) are tricky, I'm not going to lie. When perfectly ripe, they are wonderfully tart and full of cherry flavor. When even barely

ASTRINGENCY

What does astringent mean? It's more than just tart or sour. Both of those can be pleasant in food and tempered by other ingredients. Astringency, on the other hand, is rarely pleasant and cannot be tempered. Believe me, I have tried. Fruits including persimmons, cornelian cherries, silverberries, and chokeberries are astringent when picked before they are fully ripe. Taste one and you'll notice a puckering in your mouth and a fuzzy, almost tingling feeling. This is caused by tannins in the fruit that cause the cells in your mucous membranes to contract. Some foods are valued for their astringency, like black tea, red wines, and spices like cloves and cinnamon. It's not harmful, and every individual's tolerance for astringency will vary. It's a matter of degree and dosage.

underripe, they will make you pucker up with their astringency. Chokecherries are ripe when dark purple or black. Don't waste your time harvesting red chokecherries; you'll spit them out and curse yourself for not heeding my advice! Chokecherries are traditionally used in jellies, since the small pits can be strained out in the juicing process. Their juice also makes a beautiful and delicious sorbet.

Cornelian cherries (*Cornus mas*) are either deep red or yellow when ripe; this is probably why someone thought they looked like cherries, but they are not closely related. This is another tree usually grown for its flowers while the fruit remains unappreciated. Cornelian cherries are very tart and high in pectin, making them an excellent fruit for jams and jellies. They're frequently used in Middle Eastern and Eastern European cuisine—I've purchased Hungarian cornelian cherry jam and enjoyed Persian rice with cornelian cherry juice in a local restaurant. Cornelian cherries are astringent before they are fully ripe. You'll know it's time to pick when the fruit starts to fall; if you have to tug on the fruit to harvest it, that fruit is not ready, even if it's bright red. Ripe fruit will be deep red (or yellow tinged with red) and should release from the tree at the touch of your hand. Freeze the fruit whole to preserve for later.

Technically, a crabapple (*Malus* spp.) is any apple with a diameter of less than two inches; they are almost identical genetically to commercial apples. Larger crabapples (one inch or more in diameter) generally have better texture and flavor, but smaller ones can still have great flavor and lots of pectin, making them useful for jellies. So many crabapples are grown for their flowers and the fruit is left unappreciated on the trees. Yet crabapples are incredibly versatile, making excellent pickles, gorgeous fruit leather, wine, jelly, and crabapple sauce for pork chops or cake batters. If you don't have time to work with your crabapples right away, you can freeze them to use later.

Elderberries (*Sambucus* spp.) are often planted as ornamentals, valued for their large flower umbels. But many elderberries also produce delicious fruit. Red elderberry (*S. racemosa*) is an attractive plant, but its fruit isn't considered edible. It's not toxic, but it tastes awful. The blue or purple berries of some elders are worth eating, but their seeds are large, so most people juice the fruit for jellies, syrups, and wine. The fruit of cultivated purple-leaved cultivars and chartreuse-leaved cultivars is also edible. Elderberries are tannic when eaten raw, but the application of heat sweetens the flavor and makes them well worth harvesting. The only edible parts of the elderberry are its ripe fruit and flowers. All other parts may cause stomach upset.

Gooseberries (*Ribes uva-crispa*) are far more popular in Europe than in the United States for reasons I simply cannot fathom. Once, in Sweden, I was served a pie that was nothing more than gooseberries in a crust, baked with a little sugar sprinkled on top. I dream of it still, lo these many years. Wild gooseberries are thorny and hairy; they're best used as juice or pulp so you can enjoy the flavor and avoid the spikiness. Cultivated gooseberries are usually smooth and can be enjoyed right off the shrub. Gooseberry juice has enough pectin to make a good jelly, and the smooth fruit is the base for the gooseberry fool, a classic British dessert.

Mulberries (*Morus* spp.) come in several colors, but the color in the name of the mulberry tree isn't always the color of the fruit you get. The red mulberry (*M. rubra*), which is native to the United States, bears a dark purple ripe fruit that looks like the fruit of the non-native black mulberry (*M. nigra*). White mulberries (*M. alba*) may have white or dark fruit. Mulberries are ready to harvest when they drop at the slightest touch or shake of the tree. A mulberry you have to pull off its stem is not a fully ripe, sweet, or tasty mulberry. And speaking of its stem, most mulberries bring a teeny tiny bit of stem with them when harvested that you may ignore or laboriously remove from the delicate fruit, one by one, depending on personal preference and how you plan to use the fruit. For clafoutis and summer puddings, I remove the stems. For jellies and chutneys, I leave them.

Oregon grape (*Mahonia* spp.) is a popular landscape plant, and its flowers are some of the earliest to bloom in spring. It's fruit, however, is often overlooked. Ripening in late summer through fall (depending on your location and the species of *Mahonia*), the clusters of blue fruit resemble small grapes. The flavor is extremely tart, and while you should taste it raw to get acquainted with the flavor, I don't recommend it for eating straight off the plant. Combined with sugar, however, it makes an excellent jam or jelly and a magnificent dessert curd.

Pawpaws (*Asimina triloba*) are the largest fruit native to the United States, yet perhaps one of the least known. Like persimmons, they are only delicious when they are super soft, making them difficult to ship and sell. Thankfully, intrepid foragers do not depend on stores, and they rejoice when they discover a grove of pawpaws. These fruits are finicky about fruiting. They have good years and bad years, so don't give up just because the trees you found didn't produce a crop. It's worth checking every year, because the flesh of a ripe pawpaw is a magnificent, fragrant custard that you can eat with a spoon right out of its skin. I've read that pawpaw's flavor does not respond well to heat unless used in sugary desserts. Since the only thing I bake with pawpaws is crème brûlée, I have no problem with that. This fruit can be frozen whole or seeded, puréed, and frozen.

The native American **persimmon** (*Diospyros virginiana*) is smaller than its better-known Asian cousins, but when it comes to persimmons, size definitely does not matter. The flavor of a ripe American persimmon is exceptional: sweet, caramelized, and fruity. This is a fruit that is only worthwhile when soft and mushy—one of the reasons it is rarely sold commercially. Gather ripe fruit from the ground (if you can beat the animals and insects to it) or catch the fruit that falls from a barely shaken tree. Any fruit that resists the touch of your hand or requires a strong shake is not ripe, and even one or two unripe persimmons in a large batch can influence the flavor in a truly unpleasant way. You may read that persimmons should only be harvested after a frost. This isn't true. Persimmons may be ripe long before frost or well into winter depending on where you live. Whether it's August or February, if they're soft and easy to part from the branch, they're ready for harvest.

Many species of **plums** (*Prunus* spp.) are familiar cultivated fruits, but other species of plums are completely neglected as food, and this should change. Cherry plums (the fruit of purple-leaf sand cherry, *Prunus × cistena*, a popular landscape tree) produce excellent fruit. The fruit is small, tart, and the same color as the foliage, making them hard to spot at first. Flowers bloom in early spring, so a late frost can destroy the fruit crop. But in a good year, it's easy to harvest a bundle. Beach plums (*Prunus maritima*) are native to the East Coast, where they're used to make a much-loved jelly, but they are considered merely ornamental in other parts of the country. Our native Chickasaw plums (*Prunus angustifolia*) produce gorgeous, bright red fruit that makes an excellent jam. All plums can be frozen whole or cut in half, pitted, and dehydrated.

Prickly pear (*Opuntia* spp.) fruit has a flavor that resembles a sweet blend of watermelon and apples. While cultivated fruit come in several colors, wild fruit is usually red, yielding a magenta juice and pulp that is blindingly gorgeous. Prickly pears are well armed with spines and glochids,[2] so handle with

---

2. Glochids are sharp, often barbed, hair-like spines that cluster around the larger cactus spines. They look deceptively harmless. Do not be fooled.

care. I keep a pair of tongs in the back of my car for opportune harvests. Juicing prickly pear fruit lets you enjoy the flavor without fear of poking a hole in your soft palette. If pulp is what you're after, skin the fruit to remove the spines and glochids and then run it through a food mill to smooth the purée. You may freeze the fruit.

Rose hips offer the perfect excuse for *not* deadheading your roses. Once the rose flower has been pollinated, the hip (the rose fruit) forms and ripens to a lovely red or orange color, packed full of flavor and vitamin C. All rose hips are edible, but the larger hips (of *R. rugosa* and *R. canina*) are easier to work with. You may juice the hips for jelly, but if you're after the pulp (for jam or rose hip soup), you'll need to remove the large, five-pointed calyx at the base of each fruit and the many hairy seeds inside. Once cleaned, rose hips may be dried or frozen. Rose hips often persist on the plant until spring. They can still be harvested then, even if they look shriveled. The flavor of the rose hip often improves with time.

Serviceberries (*Amelanchier* spp.), also known as juneberries and Saskatoon berries, are slightly larger than blueberries. They should be harvested when they are dark blue, as the red fruit, while edible, isn't as sweet and juicy. The fruit ripens gradually over a period of several weeks; freeze your initial harvests until you have enough to work with. Serviceberries are delicious raw or in pies, puddings, jams, clafoutis, ice creams, and wine—the flavor is reminiscent of something between a strawberry and a blueberry, with a touch of almond. Dried serviceberries are delicious added to granola or pemmican. There are several species of *Amelanchier* and the flavor varies from tree to tree, so taste a berry before making a massive harvest.

Silverberry (*Elaeagnus umbellata*) is sometimes called sweet autumn olive, but don't confuse it with Russian olive, which has a very different flavor profile. Many foragers call it silverberry to avoid confusion. Silverberry is an invasive, thorny shrub that forms great thickets in the landscape. It produces abundant fruit, which often looks ripe long before it's ready to harvest. To avoid astringency, harvest when the fruit is red and slightly puckered. The flavor will still be slightly tart, but also sweet. Silverberries are high in vitamin C and lycopene, the antioxidant found in tomatoes. Use silverberry juice instead of lemon juice in a pink meringue pie, or run the fruit through a food mill and make a delicious quick bread with the pulp. The berries freeze well.

FRUIT PUDDING

This can be served on its own as a pudding, used as a pie filling, or sprinkled with your favorite crisp topping. It's a great way to showcase the flavor of the fruit without a lot of extras to get in the way, and it's so simple I almost feel guilty calling it a recipe.

YIELD: 4 ($^1/_2$-CUP) SERVINGS

2 cups foraged fruit purée

3 tablespoons instant tapioca

$^1/_3$ cup sugar

In a saucepan, stir together the purée, tapioca, and sugar and let the mixture sit for 5 minutes.

Bring the pudding to a simmer, stirring to prevent sticking, then remove the pan from the stove. If you're using a very tart fruit, like cornelian cherries or chokeberries, taste the pudding as it simmers and feel free to add more sugar, 1 tablespoon at a time, tasting between each addition.

FRUIT CHUTNEY

We expect food made with fruit to be sweet, which is why I love making fruit-based savory dishes. Surprise! This chutney combines the natural sweetness of your favorite foraged fruits with the sharpness of vinegar, the bite of onions, and a little citrus. Combined with your favorite spices, it makes a great accompaniment for meat or cheese.

Note: Booze-infused fruit from another project works well in this recipe.

YIELD: 8 (^{1}/$_2$-PINT) JARS

6 cups fruit (whole berries or roughly chopped larger fruit)

1 cup raisins (or dried serviceberries or blueberries)

^{3}/$_4$ cup chopped onion

3 tablespoons grated fresh, tropical ginger*

1^2/$_3$ cups brown sugar

1 cup apple cider vinegar

Pinch of salt

^{1}/$_4$ cup lime juice

Combine all of the ingredients in a large, heavy saucepan and bring to a simmer. Cook over low heat for at least 1 hour, stirring regularly to avoid scorching and to combine the ingredients so they meld into a chunky stew of sweet and sour deliciousness.

Check the consistency of the chutney. If the fruit isn't softened to your liking, simmer for a little longer. Chutney can be canned in a boiling water bath for long-term storage, and it keeps (without caning) in the refrigerator for months due to its high acid content.

For an easy variation, substitute 2 tablespoons of red chile powder for the raisins, and after an hour of simmering, transfer the fruit to a blender and pulverize until smooth. You have just made a foraged fruit barbecue sauce!

* I prefer tropical ginger in this recipe. It provides a brighter flavor than wild ginger, and wild ginger is a spice that should be consumed in small quantities (see page 23).

JUICE MOUSSE

You can make this light and airy dessert with any juice, but I like it best with a tart juice from fruits like wild grapes, wild plums, cornelian cherries, and Oregon grapes. Most of these fruits give you a beautifully colored juice as a bonus.

YIELD: 6 (6-OUNCE) SERVINGS

1^1/$_2$ tablespoons unflavored gelatin

^{1}/$_4$ cup cold water

2 cups foraged fruit juice

^{2}/$_3$ cup plus 1 teaspoon sugar, divided

Pinch of salt

2 tablespoons lemon juice

1 cup whipping cream (you may substitute coconut cream or a nondairy whipped topping)

2 egg whites

Sprinkle the gelatin onto the water and let it bloom for about 5 minutes (see page 33).

In a saucepan, combine the juice and ^{2}/$_3$ cup sugar over medium heat, whisking to dissolve. Add the salt and lemon juice and whisk to combine.

Next, add the bloomed gelatin to the juice. Reduce the heat to low and whisk to dissolve the gelatin. Test a bit between your fingers to be sure all the granules have dissolved, then pour the mixture into a bowl, cover, and refrigerate until the juice has begun to jell. It should be softly jelled, not fully jelled; this will take 2–3 hours.

In a separate bowl, whip the cream until it reaches the soft peak stage. If you're using whipping cream, add the teaspoon of sugar. If you're using coconut cream or another nondairy whipped topping, you probably won't need the extra sugar. Taste the cream and adjust accordingly.

Add the juice mixture and egg whites to the whipped cream and beat on high until the entire mixture is thick and evenly-colored. A stand mixer is handy for this, as it takes about 5 minutes.

Transfer the mousse into pretty dishes for individual servings or into a cookie crust for a chilled pie. Refrigerate until you're ready to serve.

CLAFOUTIS

Clafoutis is a marvelous French invention with a consistency somewhere between pudding and cake. It reminds me of a thick, moist pancake, and it could not be easier to make. You don't even need a bowl, because you make it in a blender!

Clafoutis can be made with any fruit (whole berries or chunks of larger fruits) and can be served warm or at room temperature. You might top it with a little whipped cream or ice cream for dessert, and it makes a delicious breakfast eaten plain or sprinkled with confectioners' sugar.

YIELD: 1 (8 OR 9-INCH) CLAFOUTIS

$1^{1}/_{4}$ cups milk (nut milk also works well)

$1/_{2}$ cups sugar, divided (if your fruit is very tart, like chokeberries or gooseberries, increase this to $^{2}/_{3}$ cups sugar)

3 eggs

1 tablespoon vanilla extract

$1/_{8}$ teaspoon salt

$1/_{2}$ cup flour

2 cups fruit

Preheat the oven to 350°F.

Combine the milk, half of the sugar, eggs, vanilla, salt, and flour in a blender and blend for a minute on the highest setting.

Lightly butter an 8- or 9-inch round baking dish and pour in enough batter to cover the bottom with about ¼ inch of batter. Bake for 5 minutes, or until the batter has just set but isn't baked solid. It should jiggle—but not run—when you shake the pan.

Remove the dish from the oven, spread the fruit over the batter, then sprinkle the remaining sugar over the fruit. If you're using large fruit, like plums or large crabapples, cut them into bite-sized pieces.

Pour the rest of the batter over the fruit and return the baking dish to the oven.

Bake for 45–55 minutes or until a toothpick inserted in the center comes out clean and the clafoutis is golden brown.

Clafoutis is a dessert for people who say they don't like desserts. (They're not fooling anyone. Everyone likes dessert.) The simple baked custard surrounds fresh fruit, yet doesn't overwhelm it with sweetness.

FRUIT CURD

Lemon curd is a beloved British dessert: tart, sweet, and outrageously rich. And here's a secret: you can make equally delicious fruit curds with almost any kind of juice. Serve the curd in little jars as an indulgent dessert or spread the curd on scones or toast. You might even add a layer of curd to a Pavlova (page 134) or pie before you add the fruit.

While many curd recipes call for straining, this one does not. (Thanks to Butter Wilde for sharing her technique with me.) That makes it less labor intensive, which means you'll make it more often. Score!

Note: If you're making curd with a nonacidic fruit (like prickly pear or black raspberries), you'll need to add a little lemon juice to make it set.

YIELD: 4 (1/2-CUP) SERVINGS

6 tablespoons butter, softened

1 cup sugar

2 whole eggs plus 2 egg yolks

2/3 cup foraged fruit juice

2 tablespoons lemon juice (for nonacidic fruits)

Pinch of salt

In a bowl, cream the butter and sugar together, then add the eggs and extra yolks a little bit at a time. This can all be done by hand; we're not going for light and fluffy, just well combined. Add the fruit juice and lemon juice (if needed) and stir well.

At this point, the liquid will have small chunks of solid butter in it, which may look strange to you if you've ever made a lemon curd by more traditional methods. But trust me, it's much easier this way: no straining, no double boiler, no gradual stirring of solid butter into hot liquid. Take a leap of faith—you won't be sorry.

Transfer the mixture to a saucepan with a heavy bottom and whisk over medium-low heat for 5–10 minutes. You'll need to stir constantly to avoid cooking the eggs, so don't walk away from the stove. As the butter melts, the curd will thicken. It's done when it coats the back of a spoon.

Remove the curd from the heat and stir in the pinch of salt. Allow the mixture to cool slightly before pouring it into serving dishes or storage containers. If you're serving this as a dessert, chill before serving. It will keep in the refrigerator for several weeks.

PAVLOVA

I always loved when my mother made this dessert—it seemed so fancy. But Pavlova is actually very simple, and it is the perfect way to showcase almost any fruit. You can use whole berries or chopped stone fruits. You might even combine fruit with curd or jam. It's a delicious and textural combination of crisp meringue, soft whipped cream, and flavorful fruit.

The meringue can be made several days in advance, thought it should be tightly wrapped and refrigerated. Don't assemble the Pavlova until you're ready to serve it, because once the whipped cream hits the meringue, the bottom layer starts to soften, and you want to maintain its satisfying crunch.

YIELD: 1 (8-INCH) PAVLOVA

3 egg whites

¾ cup sugar

¼ teaspoon salt

1 teaspoon white vinegar

½ teaspoon vanilla extract

1 teaspoon cornstarch

Whipped cream, to taste

2 to 3 cups foraged fruit (whole berries or roughly chopped fruit)

Spray the sides and bottoms of an 8-inch spring form pan with an oil spray that includes flour, like Baker's Joy.

Beat the egg whites until frothy. Continuing to beat, gradually add the sugar and the salt. Next, add the vinegar and vanilla, beating until the egg whites are stiff.

Sift the cornstarch onto the meringue and fold it in.

Scoop the meringue into the pan and smooth the surface. Make a slight indentation in the center, building up the sides a little.

Bake for 30 minutes, then turn off the oven and leave the meringue in for 1 hour.

When you're ready to serve, fill the meringue with whipped cream and 2–3 cups of foraged fruit, then serve immediately. As my mother wrote on the back of her recipe card: "Delicious."

Pavlova   250°

Butter for greasing an 8" or 9" spring form cake pan
  & removable bottom.

3 egg whites   1. butter bottom & sides of
3/4 C. sugar   pan. Sprinkle & flour
1/4 tsp salt   shake out excess
1 tsp white vinegar   2. line pan & round of wax
1 tsp cornstarch   paper & butter.
1/2 tsp vanilla

FRUIT FOOL

You can make a fool from almost any fruit, although gooseberry fool is generally considered to be the original fool fruit. I prefer my fools to be a little chunky, so I make them with purée rather than juice, but you could go either way. Some recipes use only fruit, sugar, and cream, but I appreciate the extra tang you get from yogurt, lemon juice, and a little white wine.

You'll need more sweetener for tart fruits like silverberry, cornelian cherries, aronia, gooseberry, and wild plums, but sweet fruits like mulberries and persimmons may not need any sweetener at all. Taste your purée before you combine it with the cream, and make your decision then.

YIELD: 4 PARFAITS

2 cups foraged fruit purée

$1/2$ cup sugar (this amount is for tart fruit; use $1/3$ cup if you're working with something sweet like brambleberries or serviceberries)

1 cup whipping cream

1 cup plain Greek yogurt

2 tablespoons lemon juice

2 tablespoons white wine

Combine the fruit purée and sugar in a saucepan and warm over medium heat, stirring to dissolve the sugar and to prevent scorching. Set this aside.

Whip the cream to stiff peaks, then gently stir in the Greek yogurt, lemon juice, and white wine.

Add half the purée to the cream, folding to combine.

Pour about 1 inch of purée into each of 4 parfait glasses, then spoon a layer of the cream/purée mix on top of the pulp. Pour a little more purée onto the cream, then repeat the cream layer. Layer until the parfait glasses are nearly full. If you'd like to add a little crunch, top the fools with your favorite foraged nut.

Some people mix together all the cream and purée, which you are certainly welcome to do. But I like how the layers look and how you dip from one layer into the next, combining cream and fruit as you go.

SUMMER PUDDING

This dessert is the perfect way to use up all your odds and ends of summer fruit. You can combine anything that pleases you (or that's lingering in your refrigerator). Traditionally, people use berries, but this recipe is equally good with stone fruits. The only requirement is that the fruit be juicy.

For the bread, use a white bread with integrity—something sturdy enough to absorb the fruit juices without falling apart. Leave the bread out on the counter for a few hours beforehand; slightly stale bread is perfect for this recipe.

I confess I was nervous about making my first summer pudding because I was afraid it wouldn't come out of the bowl. I read recipes that suggested oiling the bowl and others that suggested lining the bowl with cling film. I knew that both of these methods would probably make it easier to unmold, but I was stubborn and wanted to try it the old-fashioned way: no oil, no cling film. It came out great—don't let fear keep you from trying this recipe.

YIELD: 1 PUDDING

1 loaf white bread (You may not use the whole loaf; the amount will vary depending on the size of the bowl.)	6 cups mixed fruits Sugar, to taste

Choose a glass bowl that will hold 6 cups of fruit, or scale the recipe to fit the bowl.

Cut the crusts off several pieces of bread and line the bowl with the bread, overlapping the pieces slightly. It doesn't have to be beautiful; it just has to completely cover the bottom and sides of the bowl.

Combine the fruits in a saucepan over medium-low heat to release the juices. Taste the juice and consider how sweet you want the pudding to be. Try ½ cup of sugar for sweet brambleberries, 1 cup for tart aronia berries, and 1½ cups for super-tart cornelian cherries or Oregon grapes. Stir in the sugar, continuing to heat the fruit until the sugar dissolves. You can taste as you go, and when the fruit mixture is sweet enough, remove it from the heat.

Use a slotted spoon to transfer the fruit into the bread-lined bowl. Some recipes will tell you to pour in the juice first to soak the bottom layer of bread, but doing so risks making the bread mushy. Using a slotted spoon will still get some juice in there, and you'll save the rest to use later in the recipe.

When the bowl is full of fruit, use a few more slices of crustless white bread to cover the top of the pudding. Place a plate on top of the final bread layer and put something heavy on it (like a large can of tomatoes or a clean rock) and refrigerate for 24 hours. During this time, the bread will soak up the fruit juices.

To unmold, slide a butter knife around the top of the pudding between the bread and the bowl, then place a plate with a rim on top of the pudding, quickly turn it over, and give it a firm downward shake. The pudding will release onto the plate, and the plate's rim will keep any juices in place.

If the bread is not completely colored by fruit juices (there may be a few white patches that have not become juicy), pour the leftover juice over the bread. Cut into the pudding to reveal the delicious wild fruits inside.

Serve plain, with whipped cream, or with custard sauce.

FRUIT QUICK BREAD

Why should bananas have all the fun? You can make a tasty quick bread with almost any kind of fruit pulp, although you may need to adjust your sweetener and spices depending on the fruit you use. Silverberry and persimmon pulp combine well with ground spicebush berries, and crabapples are nice with ground wild ginger.

YIELD: 1 (9 X 5-INCH) LOAF

1 stick unsalted butter, softened	$^1/_2$ teaspoon salt
$^3/_4$ cup sugar	$1^1/_2$ teaspoons ground, dried spicebush berries (or ground, dried wild ginger)
1 egg	
2 cups flour	
1 teaspoon baking powder	1 cup foraged fruit purée
1 teaspoon baking soda	1 teaspoon vanilla extract

Preheat the oven to 375°F.

Cream the butter and sugar, then add the egg and combine thoroughly. Set aside.

Combine the flour, baking powder, baking soda, salt, and ground spicebush berries (or ginger), then blend them into the butter mixture.

Add the fruit purée and vanilla to the other ingredients and mix thoroughly. The batter will be quite stiff.

Spoon the batter into a greased 5 x 9-inch loaf pan and bake for 50 minutes or until a toothpick inserted in the center comes out clean.

Remove the cake from the pan when it is cool enough to handle. Let it cool on a rack.

Fruity quick breads are most delicious when lightly toasted and buttered. Serve them with tea in the afternoon or as a special breakfast. For dessert, drizzle a simple confectioners' sugar icing over the top of the loaf.

SPICEBUSH MACARONS
WITH CRABAPPLE BUTTER

My macarons don't look like store-bought macarons, but I'll enter them in a flavor contest with the pros any day! Macarons somehow manage to be light and airy (thanks to the egg whites) and richly sweet (thanks to the butter and sugar) at the same time. This is a compelling cookie.

If you don't have a pastry bag, use a large Ziplock bag with the corner cut off. (That's what I did before I decided to make macarons on a regular basis.) And if the feet (the ruffled edges of the macarons) of your cookies spread a little too wide or the tops of your cookies crack, don't worry—they'll still be delicious.

YIELD: 40 TO 50 MACARONS

FOR THE COOKIES
1 cup confectioners' sugar

³/₄ cup almond flour

1 tablespoon dried, ground spicebush berries

2 egg whites

¼ cup granulated sugar

1 teaspoon vanilla extract

FOR THE FILLING
¼ cup butter

¼ cup thick crabapple purée

⅓ cup brown sugar

2 tablespoons milk

1 tablespoon dried, ground spicebush berries

Confectioners' sugar

Line 2 baking sheets with parchment paper or silicone baking sheets.

Sift together the confectioners' sugar, almond flour, and ground spicebush berries. I often skip the sifting step in baking, but it's important for macarons. Throw away any bits that are too big to coax through the strainer, then sift the mixture again and set it aside.

Beat the egg whites until frothy. (Use a stand mixer if possible, because you're going to be beating these whites for a long time.) Add the granulated sugar, a little at a time, then add the vanilla. Beat the whites on high for about 5 minutes. The whites should be so stiff that when you turn the bowl upside down, they don't budge.

Sift the almond flour mixture into the egg whites and fold together. This may be the most critical step in the whole process. The ingredients take a while to integrate, but

continued

keep at it. They will eventually combine into a glossy, viscous batter. Stop when you can drop a ribbon of batter from the spatula into the bowl and the ribbon disappears within 30 seconds.

Fill the pastry bag (or Ziplock with the corner cut off) with the batter and pipe circles of batter onto the silicone mat. The cookies will expand a little, so aim for circles of batter that are about 1½ inches wide and be sure to give each cookie about 1 inch on either side to expand. Don't worry about making perfect circles. That is *so* much less important than the flavor.

When the baking sheets are full, drop each sheet onto the counter from a height of about 6 inches. Do this 3–4 times to smack the air bubbles out of the batter. Let the baking sheets sit at room temperature for about 30 minutes so they form a skin on top— the tops will look shiny and your finger won't leave a mark if you gently poke a cookie.

While you wait, preheat the oven to 300°F.

I found all sorts of baking times for macarons, ranging from 12–20 minutes. Much will depend on your oven and the size of the cookies. I bake mine for 18 minutes, giving each baking sheet a half turn at the 9 minute mark. The cookies should *not* brown, and they should lift easily from the parchment paper or silicone sheet. If they stick, give them another 1–2 minutes in the oven.

When the cookies are done, let them cool completely while you make the filling.

Most commercial macarons are filled with ganache or buttercream; I use a combination of butter and crabapple purée. It's got the same creamy consistency as buttercream, but a fruitier, foraged flavor and a lovely, natural color. The purée should be thick enough to stick to a spoon, so if yours is more fluid, strain it to eliminate as much liquid as possible.

Melt the butter in a small saucepan, then add the crabapple purée and brown sugar. Bring the mixture to a boil, stirring to prevent sticking. Lower the heat to a simmer, and continue to stir 2 minutes.

Add the milk and ground spicebush berries, continuing to stir and simmer for 1 minute. Remove the mixture from the heat and allow it to cool to room temperature. You should be able to touch the outside of the pot and have it feel neither hot nor cold.

Add confectioners' sugar in increments until the filling is thick enough to spread. I use ¼ cup, and while it is still a little runny, I prefer to let the filling continue to cool until it reaches the right consistency instead of adding more sugar.

While the filling cools, turn all the cookies upside down. Using a knife or spoon, spread a dollop of filling on half of the cookies, then place a plain cookie on top of each frosted cookie to make a sandwich.

Apparently macarons should be refrigerated for 24 hours to reach the right consistency, and they really do get better overnight. (The cookies soften ever so slightly as they meld with the filling.) But I've never been able to resist eating one right away. After all, that's part of the job: quality control.

PAWPAW
CRÈME BRÛLÉE

You don't really have to do anything to a pawpaw to make it delicious, but if you want to take this foraged fruit over the top, try pawpaw crème brûlée. You'll need a cup of purée for this recipe, which should require either 2 medium or 3 small pawpaws.

YIELD: 4 SERVINGS

2 cups heavy cream

2 tablespoons bourbon

2/3 cup sugar plus more for the tops of the custards

1/8 teaspoon salt

5 egg yolks (save the whites for a Pavlova (page 134) or add them to your next omelet or scramble)

1 cup pawpaw purée

Preheat the oven to 350°F.

Combine the cream and bourbon in a saucepan and bring it just to a simmer. Whisk to prevent scorching. Remove it from the heat as soon as the first bubbles appear and set it aside.

Whisk the sugar and salt into the egg yolks. Add the heated cream mixture to the eggs, a little at a time, whisking constantly. This is called tempering the eggs; the goal is to raise the temperature of the eggs without cooking them. If you add too much hot liquid too quickly, the eggs will cook and solidify rather than form a silky, thickened liquid. It's easier than it sounds, as long as you proceed slowly and carefully.

Stir in the pawpaw purée and combine thoroughly.

Pour the custard mixture into 4 (3-inch) ramekins and place the ramekins in a shallow roasting pan. Fill the pan with water to within a half inch of the top of the ramekins, then bake for about 30 minutes. The tops of the custards should not be entirely solid when you take them out of the oven; they should look a little jiggly.

Refrigerate the custards overnight or for at least 4–6 hours.

Before serving, sprinkle a layer of sugar on top of each custard (about 1 tablespoon per ramekin). Then, using a small torch, melt the sugar and let it cool (briefly!) to form that glassy, sweet topping that cracks so satisfyingly under a gentle whap from your spoon.

Do not kid yourself thinking there will be leftovers and you might save one pawpaw crème brûlée for breakfast. There will never be leftovers.

Spiced Nut Mix (page 160)

NUTS
AND SEEDS

· ·

What's the difference between a nut and a seed?
Botanically speaking, a seed is an embryonic plant
enclosed within a protective coat, like a mustard seed
or an elm samara.[1] A nut is a dry fruit with a seed
inside, like an acorn or a chestnut. To make matters
even more confusing, several things we consider
culinary nuts (walnuts, hickory nuts) are botanically
classified as drupes, or drupaceous nuts. (Is your head
spinning yet?) All nuts contain seeds, but not all seeds
come from nuts. Fortunately, you don't need to know
any of that to enjoy the recipes in this chapter.

---

1. A samara is a seed enclosed in a papery covering, like a maple helicopter.

Fall is the primary season for nuts, but a few nuts ripen in summer, and others have multiple harvest seasons. Seeds ripen throughout the growing season. Some are best eaten fresh and others dried. While we never eat the hard shell of a nut, some seed coverings can be eaten, while others are removed.

Special Equipment

Because nuts and seeds often come with layers of protection, they may require special equipment to access their deliciousness. My first teacher in horticultural school told me to buy the best tools I could afford, and from my first purchase—a pair of Felco pruners—to the Davebilt nutcracker I use for my acorns, that advice has stood me in good stead. Having the right tool for the job makes cooking wild food much easier, and if something is easier, you'll do it more often, right?

The **Davebilt nutcracker** is handmade in California. It's intended to crack hazelnuts, almonds, and English walnuts, but it works wonderfully for acorns, too. The hopper (where you pour the nuts) has an adaptable opening, so you can adjust it to fit the size of the nut you're cracking. Once the nuts are cracked, you'll need to shell them, but this is easily accomplished with a nut pick. If you get serious about working with acorns (and I highly recommend you do), the Davebilt will save you hours of time over cracking your acorns with a hammer.

Black walnuts require their own special tool. Their shells are terrifically hard, and old timers will regale you with stories of driving trucks over the nuts to crack the shells. I recommend a special, black walnut cracker like Grandpa's Goody Getter or the Kenkel Cracker. Do not try to crack a black walnut with anything other than a black walnut cracker. It will only end in tears and injury.

I don't think a hammer counts as specialized equipment, but it works on many nuts. If you're just starting out, you probably don't want to invest in a lot of equipment. When cracking nuts with a hammer, you'll also need a board and a few sacrificial dish towels. Place the board on a stable, flat surface and lay a dish towel on top of the board. Spread a few nuts on the dish towel, cover with another dish towel, then go to town with the hammer. This works well for ginkgo nuts, acorns, and apricot kernels. It also works for pine nuts, but you'll need a very light touch, since pine nut shells are thin and the nut meats are soft.

The dry grains container of my Vitamix is a wonderful tool. The blade is specially designed to turn grain into flour; whether you're grinding wheat berries or dried chestnuts, the dry grains container makes short work of it.

Preserving the Harvest

Nuts and seeds contain more fat than most plants we forage for. That's handy when you're looking for calories, but since fat spoils quickly, you can't leave your nuts and seeds sitting around on the counter. You'll either need to work with them quickly or preserve them.

FREEZING

Nuts can be frozen in the shell or after shelling. I often freeze bags of whole fresh acorns and chestnuts in autumn, then shell them in winter when I have more time to play with my harvest. If I'm still not ready to cook with them, I pop them right back in the freezer.

DEHYDRATION

If you plan to use your nuts for flour (acorns and chestnuts), you'll need to dry them before grinding. I dry shelled nuts at 105°F until they are so hard that I can't break them in half by hand. You can then store them in an airtight container in the freezer or on the shelf. Don't grind them until you're ready to use the flour; the nuts will oxidize more quickly once they've been ground.

When making flour from dry dock seeds, I don't bother to dehydrate them for two reasons. First, they're already pretty darn dry when I harvest them from the plant, and second, I roast them before turning them into flour, which not only improves the flavor but also gets rid of any residual moisture.

PRESSING

Most foragers, including myself, don't have an oil press. But many nuts make excellent oils, and if you get seriously into self-sufficiency, this may be something you'd like to try. My friends Melissa Price and Sam Thayer make a delicious hickory nut oil which they sell at their store, The Forager's Harvest. Acorns also make an excellent oil. Remember when I said nuts contain lots of fat? That's why they make good oils.

General Techniques

ALCOHOL

You might be surprised at how many nut liqueurs there are—and how many you can make that are far better than anything you can buy in a store. Even if you're not interested in alcoholic beverages, you might want to try making your own extracts.

Did you know that almond extract is actually made from apricot kernels (page 167)? You can take it a step further and turn your extract into *noyaux*, a superb almond-flavored liqueur. You can make extracts using the same technique with pine nuts, hickory nuts, or acorns, but remember that anything made with acorns requires an extra step: leaching out the bitter tannins (see sidebar on page 152).

FLOUR

Several nuts and seeds make excellent flours, but since they don't contain gluten, they won't bind or rise like wheat flours. That's why most nut and seed flours should only be substituted for ¼ to ½ of the flour in bread and cake recipes. Cookies, crackers, and brownies can be made exclusively with nut or seed flours, but they'll be more crumbly than what you're used to.

Any nut or seed you intend to grind should be thoroughly dried before grinding. If you don't have a Vitamix or a special flour mill, you can use a spice grinder to make small batches of flour.

Seasonal Availability

	Spring	Summer	Fall	Winter
acorns (*Quercus* spp.)			X	
apricot kernels (*Prunus armeniaca*)		X		
black walnuts (*Juglans nigra*)	X	X	X	
chestnuts (*Castanea dentata*)			X	
dock seeds (*Rumex* spp.)		X	X	
ginkgo nuts (*Ginkgo biloba*)			X	X
hickory nuts (*Carya* spp.)			X	
mustard seeds (*various species*)	X	X	X	
pine nuts (*Pinus edulis*)			X	
Siberian elm samaras (*Ulmus pumila*)	X			

Acorns are a rite of passage for many foragers, and as such, they get extra real estate here. Before my first attempt at cooking with acorns, I was intimidated by what I perceived to be an enormous amount of work. Boy, is it worth it! An excellent and ample wild source of fat and protein, acorn populations fluctuate from years of great abundance (mast years) to years of great scarcity. I try to harvest enough in mast years to get me through the lean years. But cooking with acorns does require an extra step. All acorns contain tannins to varying degrees, which not only give the nuts a bitter flavor, it also limits how well your intestines absorb nutrients. While red acorns are generally considered more bitter than white acorns, I don't factor this into my harvest. I look for the largest acorns to maximize the amount of nut meats I collect and minimize the amount of work I have to do to enjoy those

PROCESSING ACORNS: HOT LEACHING VERSUS COLD LEACHING

Leaching is the process of removing tannins from acorns by drawing them out with water. When choosing between hot leaching and cold leaching, consider how you're going to use the acorns. If you're going to use them as flour in baked goods, cold leaching is the way to go. If you're going to use them in soups or as nuts, hot leaching is faster and easier. But hot leaching cooks the starch in the acorns, so they'll require an extra binder to hold together—which is why cold leaching is a better choice if you're intending to bake with acorn flour.

Before you leach the acorns, taste an unleached nut. It will be bitter, but it will give you a baseline to monitor your progress during the leaching process.

Hot Leaching

To hot leach acorns, fill a large pot ⅓ full with shelled nuts, then add enough water to cover the nuts by a few inches. Bring the water to a boil, cook until the water turns dark brown, then pour off the water. Repeat the process several times.

You may read that you should continue to boil until the water stays clear, but that doesn't always happen. The water may look brown long after all bitterness has been leached from the nuts. Start tasting the acorns after the third or fourth change of water. When there's no trace of bitterness, your nuts are leached. Depending on the acorn, this could take as many as 15 changes of water.

You may also read that acorns must be moved from one pot of boiling water to another, rather than out of boiling water into cold water that is then brought to the boil. Some foragers swear that cold water sets the tannins in the nuts, making them permanently bitter, but I've done it both ways and I can't say there's a difference.

nut meats! You'll have to decide whether to hot leach or cold leach the tannins from the nuts, and to do this, you'll need to know how you plan to use the acorns.

You might consider apricots (*Prunus armeniaca*) to be a cultivated crop—they certainly are. But where I live, they're a common street tree, and the sidewalks are littered with fallen fruit in good years. People put signs out in front of their houses begging people to pick the fruit, and as an urban forager, I'm happy to oblige. The fruit is delicious, but the kernels inside the apricot pits, packed with almond flavor, are a hidden prize. I collect them in a bag and freeze them until I have enough to work with—these seeds are best accessed with a hammer, and the kernels are easier to crack when frozen. Don't worry if the kernels are a little crushed; they still make a great infusion.

After boiling, hot-leached acorns will be darker in color than cold-leached acorns. They can be coarsely ground and used as nuts in baked goods, and they make an excellent soup.

Cold Leaching

There are several methods of cold leaching. I've personally tried four, and this is my favorite—not only is it effective, it's fast.

Cold-leached acorns can be ground into a fine flour or a coarse polenta. Acorn flour doesn't have gluten in it, so it won't rise on its own. That's why you'll often see recipes calling for equal parts acorn flour and wheat flour. Some baked goods, like cookies, crackers, and brownies, work well with cold-leached acorn flour alone. The starch you preserve by cold leaching helps bind the baked goods.

The running water method is the fastest way to cold leach the acorns. It's also the most labor-intensive method, but it is by no means difficult. Put a cup of shelled nuts in a blender and add enough water to cover the nuts by four to five inches. Pulverize to create a slurry, then set aside.

Place a large colander in the sink and line it with a dish towel. Pour the slurry into the colander, then run cool water into the colander and stir with a large spoon. After eight minutes of stirring, taste the slurry. If there is any bitter flavor, let the water run for another two or three minutes and taste again. You should be able to stir without spilling, which is why this is best done in small batches in a large colander. Once the acorn slurry is not at all bitter, squeeze out as much excess water as possible. You can dry this in a dehydrator or use the flour when it's still damp. If you do the latter, use a little less liquid in your recipe.

Black walnuts have two harvest seasons. (Thank you, *Juglans nigra*!) In late spring and early summer, immature black walnuts make an excellent liqueur (page 168). The flavor of black walnuts is winey and dark, unlike any other nut I know. But a word of caution: while you may have enjoyed pickled walnuts (a British pub classic), don't waste your time or walnuts trying this recipe with black walnuts; it doesn't work. I've tried multiple times, and every forager I know who has tried the recipe with black walnuts agrees. The texture is grainy and unpleasant. In autumn, black walnuts fall, littering the ground with what look like green tennis balls. Remove the husks by hand (wear gloves—the husks stain skin black), then dry the nuts for a few days before shelling them in your special black walnut nutcracker.

Chestnuts (*Castanea dentata*) can be enjoyed so many ways: roasted and eaten whole, dried and ground into flour for baking, boiled and puréed to make creamy soups and mousses, baked into stuffing. Chestnut blight hit the American chestnut hard; you're more likely to find feral Asian chestnuts in the wild these days, and while they're not quite as sweet, they're still tasty and worth harvesting. Leave the spiky outer husks behind; they've usually split open by the time the nuts fall from the tree. To remove the thin, inner shell, make an X on the flat side of each nut with a serrated knife. Place the chestnuts on a baking sheet and roast for 25 minutes at 400°F. Opening the skin of the nut allows steam to escape and prevents the chestnuts from exploding in the oven. The skin peels back from the X and comes off easily when the nuts are still warm. Peeling becomes more difficult as the nuts cool, but you can always zap them in the microwave to rewarm them.

Dock plants (*Rumex* spp.) are common weeds, usually foraged for their plentiful and tasty greens (page 82). By early to mid-summer, the tall, branching spikes of small green flowers have given way to hundreds of orange-brown seeds, making the plants easy to spot from a distance. Each seed is enclosed in a tightly fitting, papery casing. Don't waste your time trying to remove the seeds from the casing; it will only lead to frustration and much cursing. Harvest them easily with the paper casing by running your hand along the stem. Spread them out on a baking sheet and roast them at 350°F for 5 minutes. This not only dries the seeds, it also sweetens them slightly. Dock seeds are slightly bitter, but in a good way, like coffee. The flour is great in brownies and crackers. Refrigerate them whole until you're ready to use the seeds, then grind them, paper casing and all.

Ginkgo nuts (*Ginkgo biloba*) are surrounded by very smelly fruit. Some people call it stinko ginkgo—the smell really is pretty bad. But get rid of that flesh and you'll be rewarded with a very tasty seed. Wait until the fruit falls to the ground in autumn, then, wearing disposable gloves, pick up the fruit and squeeze the seed into a plastic bag, leaving the smelly flesh behind. I wear gloves to keep the stink off my hands, but I've read that ginkgo flesh can cause a skin rash, so gloves are a doubly good idea. That said, I've harvested bare-handed and never had a problem, and none of my foraging friends have reported issues. Wash away any fleshy remnants clinging to the seeds. Cleaned seeds can then be frozen in their shells for later use. Ginkgo nuts are mild and soft. They're often used in Asian soups and desserts to add contrasting texture, and they make a great fried bar snack. The crispy outside contrasts nicely with the creamy inside. Ginkgo nuts should only be eaten cooked, not raw, and in limited quantities, though there is debate about how many nuts are safe to eat. Adults are currently advised to eat no more than 8 nuts at a time, but years ago, when no such recommendations were in place, I ate 20 to 30 nuts in a sitting multiple times. I'm not saying you should do this, but I do encourage you to do your own research.

There are several species of hickory (*Carya* spp.) that produce tasty nuts. Pecans (*C. illinoinensis*) are probably the best known, although their native range is smaller than some of our other native hickories. Shagbark hickory (*C. ovata*) and pignut hickory (*C. glabra*) are both very flavorful and more widespread. Hickory nuts vary greatly both in size and in the hardness of their shells. Both pignuts and shagbark hickory nuts are relatively easy to shell. Picking the nutmeats out of their shells requires patience, but it's worth the work. The flavor of a freshly shelled pignut is similar to that of pecans, but slightly sweeter.

There are many different kinds of mustard seeds with varying degrees of spiciness. Mustard seeds are borne in capsules called siliques, which are long and thin. These capsules will split open and disperse their contents, so be sure to harvest when the pods look dry but before they split open. The seeds can be used to make mustard (page 166) or to flavor breads and crackers. A good general rule is that the darker the seed, the spicier the flavor. Black mustard seeds are the spiciest, followed by brown mustard seeds. White seeds are generally the mildest. All mustard seeds are edible.

Have you ever wondered why pine nuts (*Pinus edulis, P. monophylla*) are so expensive? If you've ever harvested and processed them, you know the answer!

Like acorns, pine nuts have mast years and years of scarcity. In early fall, the scales of mature cones open up, letting the seeds fall to the ground—but some foragers don't wait for this to happen. You can harvest unopened cones and let them open at home—roasting the cones speeds up the opening. Only then does the hard work begin—pine nuts have very thin shells! While some people pop unshelled nuts in their mouths, crack the shells with their teeth, and spit out the shells, I'm not one of those people. I love the flavor of pine nuts, but processing the small, soft seeds is a lot of work.

Siberian elms (*Ulmus pumila*) are weed trees, plain and simple. In most locations, the millions (no exaggeration) of seeds they produce every spring result in overwhelming numbers of weed tree seedlings. Elm seeds are enclosed in round papery coverings called samaras. Before they dry and fall off the tree, clogging your gutters and sprouting wherever they can find a foothold, Siberian elm samaras have a delectable nutty, sweet flavor. They make a tasty trail nibble and are great in egg dishes. I like them best mixed in with rice or pasta, garnished with a little goat cheese.

Elm samaras

FORAGED NUT ICE CREAM MASTER RECIPE

I think ice cream is always improved by contrasting textures, which is why I love nut ice creams. The combination of flavorful crunch with smooth creaminess makes a good thing even better. Different nuts go well with different ice cream bases, but I suggest starting out with a sweet cream or vanilla base to really focus on the flavor of the featured nut. Once you've done that, there's no reason you can't play around. Try black walnuts in chocolate or pine nuts with *dulce de leche*.

YIELD: 3 CUPS

1 cup milk

1 cup heavy cream

$^1/_2$ cup sugar

2 pinches of sea salt, divided

$^1/_2$ cup chopped black walnuts (or hickory nuts, ginkgo nuts, pine nuts)

$^1/_2$ vanilla bean, split (or $^1/_2$ teaspoon vanilla extract)

2 egg yolks

Combine the milk, cream, sugar, 1 pinch of salt, and nuts in a saucepan and heat until the liquid begins to steam but not simmer. Remove from the heat, scrape the seeds of the split vanilla bean into the liquid, add the shell of the vanilla bean, and let the whole thing cool for 1 hour.

Strain off the nuts and vanilla bean shell. Discard the shell and refrigerate the nuts in an airtight container.

Reheat the milk and cream, once again bringing it to the steaming (but not simmering) point. As the cream is warming, beat the egg yolks and the remaining salt in an electric mixer until they are light yellow. Pour a few tablespoons of the hot cream mixture into the egg yolks, whisking the yolks constantly. The slow introduction of hot liquid to egg yolks is called tempering. If you add the hot ingredients to the eggs all at once, you risk cooking the eggs, causing small bits of solid egg to form in the batter.

Once you've tempered the yolks, add them to the remainder of the cream, and whisk to combine thoroughly. Pour the batter into a container, cover, and refrigerate the mixture until it's thoroughly cold (at least 4–5 hours or overnight).

Transfer the mixture to your ice cream maker and freeze as directed. About 5 minutes before the end of the freezing cycle, add in the reserved nuts that you used to infuse the cream. The ice cream can be eaten as soft serve right away or stored in the freezer for several hours to harden up.

CHOCOLATE NUT CANDY

This recipe is ridiculously simple and no one can eat just one. If the idea of using store-bought chocolate chips doesn't appeal to you, feel free to make your own chocolate. Personally, I appreciate the ease of working with chocolate chips; I have no desire to temper my own chocolate.[2] This recipe works with any nut of choice.

YIELD: 30 TO 40 CANDIES

½ cup foraged nuts

2 cups chocolate chips

1 tablespoon sea salt

Roughly chop the foraged nuts.

Using a double boiler, melt the chocolate chips. You can also do this in a microwave, using 30-second intervals to gradually melt the chocolate.

Stir the chopped nuts into the melted chocolate, then transfer spoonfuls of the chocolate nut mixture to a sheet of waxed paper. Use your fingers to sprinkle a mini-pinch of sea salt on top of each chocolate, then let the chocolate sit long enough to solidify.

I told you it was simple! I'm especially fond of this candy made with California bay nuts, because their slightly bitter flavor perfectly balances the sweet chocolate and whisper of salt. It's also excellent with pine nuts and hickory nuts.

---

2. Tempering chocolate is different from tempering eggs. Tempering gives chocolate a shiny, even surface. It requires heating and then cooling melted chocolate to very specific temperatures, and the whole idea makes me nervous. What if I let the chocolate cool to 83°F instead of 82°F? Do I have to start all over again?!

SPICED NUT MIX

My sister Elizabeth is not a forager, but she is a very good cook, and every year she makes big batches of spiced pecans as holiday gifts. I've tinkered with her spice mix just a little (to add a few foraged spices) and used it with a mix of foraged nuts. It's a great way to use up odds and ends of wild nuts after making the big, show-stopping recipes. Note: acorns aren't great in this recipe, but it works well with pine nuts, black walnuts, hickory nuts, and ginkgo nuts.

YIELD: 4 CUPS

1 egg white

$1/4$ cup sugar

1 teaspoon salt

$1/2$ teaspoon red chili powder

$1 1/2$ tablespoons cayenne powder

$1/8$ teaspoon unsweetened cocoa powder

$1/8$ teaspoon field garlic powder or powdered ramps

$1/4$ teaspoon ground spicebush berries

4 cups foraged nuts

Preheat the oven to 300°F.

Beat the egg white until foamy. In a separate bowl, combine all of the spices, then whisk them into the beaten egg white. Stir in the nuts until they are well coated.

Spread the coated nuts in a single layer on an ungreased baking sheet and bake for 15 minutes. Remove the sheet from the oven and use a metal spatula to separate and flip the nuts. Return to the oven for another 10 minutes.

Remove from the oven, stir the nuts around again, and let them cool on the baking sheet. Once they're cool, break up the clumps and store them in an airtight jar for up to 2 weeks.

BROWNIES

This recipe can be made with acorn flour, chestnut flour, or dock seed flour. Each one brings something special to the table. Dock flour is slightly bitter and balances the sweetness of chocolate. Acorn flour is rich and dark, and chestnut flour is mild and sweet.

Just as you can vary the foraged flour, so too can you vary the foraged nuts. The strong flavor of black walnuts holds its own alongside acorn flour, while milder pine nuts and hickory nuts are better with chestnut flour. Dock flour and California bay nuts make an especially tasty flavor combination.

YIELD: 1 (8 X 8-INCH) PAN

2 ounces unsweetened baking chocolate	1 tablespoon dried, ground spicebush berries
$\frac{1}{2}$ cup unsalted butter	$\frac{1}{2}$ teaspoon vanilla extract
$\frac{7}{8}$ cup sugar	2 eggs
$\frac{3}{8}$ cup dock seed flour	$\frac{1}{4}$ cup chopped California bay nuts (or nut of choice)
$\frac{1}{8}$ teaspoon salt	

Preheat the oven to 350°F.

Melt the chocolate and butter together in a double boiler or in the microwave.

In a mixing bowl, combine the sugar, flour, salt, and ground spicebush berries. Add the chocolate, vanilla, and eggs, mixing to create a thick batter. Add the chopped nuts and stir to combine.

Spread the batter evenly in an 8 x 8-inch greased baking pan.

Bake for 20–30 minutes, or until a toothpick inserted in the center of the brownies comes out clean. Let the pan cool for at least 30 minutes before cutting into the brownies; they need to cool and set.

This recipe is easy to double if you have lots of mouths to feed—or if you just really like brownies.

CRABAPPLE CAKE

I first made this with a mix of acorn and traditional wheat flours, and since then I've tried it with several different combinations. It works very well with chestnut flour in the same proportions described below. If you try it with dock seed flour, use $^1\!/_2$ cup foraged flour and increase the traditional flour to $1^1\!/_2$ cups.

You may also substitute for the crabapple purée. I've used pear, flowering quince, plum, and apricot, and all are delicious. Finally, you may substitute olive oil for the coconut oil. The hint of coconut from the oil comes through in this recipe, which I like. But I know coconut can be a polarizing flavor, so if you're not a fan, try olive oil.

YIELD: 1 BUNDT CAKE

1 cup cold-leached acorn flour	2 teaspoons ground spicebush berries
1 cup traditional wheat flour (or gluten-free flour mix)	6 eggs
1 teaspoon baking soda	1 cup coconut oil (or olive oil)
1 teaspoon baking powder	1 cup honey
$^1\!/_2$ teaspoon salt	$^3\!/_4$ cup crabapple purée
1 cup sugar	Confectioners' sugar, for dusting

Preheat the oven to 350°F, then grease and flour a Bundt pan.

In a mixing bowl, combine the flours, baking soda, baking powder, salt, sugar, and ground spicebush berries. No sifting required; just stir everything together well.

In a second bowl, beat the eggs, coconut oil, honey, and crabapple purée. Since coconut oil may be either solid or liquid (depending on room temperature), the batter may be either perfectly smooth or contain small chunks. Either way is ok, but with solid coconut oil, beat the batter enough that any chunks are no bigger than ¼–½ inch.

Combine the dry and liquid ingredients, then transfer the batter to the Bundt pan.

Bake for 30–40 minutes, or until a skewer inserted into the center of the cake comes out clean. Let the cake cool in the pan for 5–10 minutes, then turn out onto a plate. Let it cool completely before dusting with confectioners' sugar.

| **NOTE:** This recipe is equally good topped with Foraged Nut Ice Cream (page 157).

BAKLAVA

I've been making baklava since before I hit puberty, but I'm not sure I'd have thought to make a foraged version if Sharon Hahn hadn't suggested it in one of my wild foods cooking classes. The teacher learns from the student.

For more than 40 years, I've made baklava in a sheet pan, filled it with walnuts, cinnamon, and nutmeg, and topped it with cloves. I do not use honey in my syrup, I prefer many light layers of filling to fewer thick layers, and I use a fine grind for my nuts. That's how my *yiayia* made baklava, and that's how I like it.

That being said, *Yiayia* might *not* appreciate my foraged acorn baklava. Not just because I'm messing with the family recipe—acorns were famine food in much of Greece, and thus a reminder of tough times. Tough times breed strong people, and my *yiayia* was a strong woman and a wonderful cook.

My first attempt at acorn baklava was a miserable failure; the acorns were so hard I was afraid I'd crack a tooth. I used hot-leached nuts for this recipe. When I hot leach acorns, I dry them afterwards to extend their shelf life. But nuts preserved this way are very hard, and they did not soften up in the baking process. I remembered that the acorns had been pleasantly soft straight out of the leaching water, so I thought soaking the nut meats overnight might soften them up. Worked like a charm.

I made this baklava as a *saragli*, a rolled baklava, but you could certainly make a sheet pan baklava with the same ingredients.

YIELD: 25 TO 30 PIECES

FOR THE PASTRIES
2 cups leached, softened acorn meats (about 1½ cups when ground)

½ cup sugar

2 tablespoons dried, ground spicebush berries

1 package commercial phyllo dough

Butter spray

FOR THE SYRUP
2 cups sugar

1¼ cups water

Peel of ½ orange

1 tablespoon dried, ground spicebush berries

2 tablespoons lemon juice

continued

Preheat the oven to 350°F.

In a food processor, pulse the acorns to a medium-fine grind. There should be some texture, but no big chunks. Transfer the nuts to a bowl, add the sugar and ground spicebush berries, and stir to combine. Set the bowl aside.

Unwrap and unroll the phyllo dough. Take a clean dish towel, soak it thoroughly with water, squeeze out the excess, then drape it over the unrolled phyllo. The moisture in the towel will keep the dough pliable. Otherwise, because phyllo dough is so thin, it can dry out and crumble faster than you might imagine.

Phyllo dough comes in various sizes, but is usually in the neighborhood of 13 x 18 inches. Cut the dough to be 1 inch larger than your pan both lengthwise and crosswise. I use a 9 x 13-inch pan and cut my phyllo to 10 x 14 inches.

Thoroughly coat the pan with butter spray[3] and set it aside.

Lay a sheet of the trimmed phyllo on a clean cutting board and spray lightly with the butter spray. Place another piece of phyllo on top of the first and spray again. Add a third sheet and spray it also. Sprinkle ¼ cup of the nut mixture across the short edge of the phyllo and roll the dough, starting at the bottom. Keep the roll as tight as possible. Turn the roll so the seam is facing down, then, holding the roll at each end, push the ends in toward each other, gently scrunching up the roll, giving it a wrinkled appearance. Then place the roll in the pan. (This is why you cut the phyllo dough slightly larger than the pan. Once you scrunch the roll, it should fit the pan perfectly.

Repeat the above process for as long as the phyllo and nut mixture last. When all the pastries are in the pan, spray the tops heavily with butter spray and cut the rolls into smaller lengths (2–3 inches long). Bake for 30 minutes at 350°F, then reduce the heat to 300°F and bake for another 30 minutes.

While the pastries are in the oven, make the syrup. In a saucepan, combine the sugar, water, orange peel, and ground spicebush berries. Whisk over medium heat to dissolve the sugar and let the syrup simmer for a few minutes. Add the lemon juice, remove the pan from the heat, and allow the syrup to cool.

After 1 hour in the oven, the acorn baklava should be golden brown. Remove from the over, pour the syrup evenly over the pastries, and let the baklava absorb the syrup for at least an hour before serving. Store, covered, in the refrigerator; they'll keep for 2 weeks.

NOTE: If you make this recipe with pine nuts or hickory nuts, you can skip the leaching and soaking.

---

3. No, *Yiayia* did not use butter spray. But I'm sure she'd appreciate how it reduces the risk of tearing the phyllo, which happens far too often when you use a brush to apply a coating of butter to the pastry.

MUSTARD

Making your own mustard is so simple. Once you've done it, you'll wonder why it took you so long to try. Here are a few basics:

The spiciness of mustard seeds varies greatly, so chew on a seed or two before you get started to assess the spiciness of your harvested seeds. You'll need to really chew up the seed and let it sit in your mouth for a minute or two to get an idea of its flavor.

The spiciness of the mustard also depends on the kind of liquid you add and when you add it to the ground mustard seeds. Combining water with ground mustard seeds initiates a chemical reaction that releases the mustard's spicy flavor, but this fades quickly over time. An initially spicy mustard and water mixture may be quite bland after sitting for several hours. To preserve the spiciness, add an acid, like vinegar, wine, or lemon juice.

Mustard thickens with time—don't worry if it seems thin at first. It should thicken up within 12 hours and be easily spreadable.

YIELD: 3 OUNCES

2 tablespoons mustard seeds	$\frac{1}{2}$ tablespoon honey
$\frac{1}{2}$ tablespoon water	$\frac{1}{4}$ teaspoon salt
$\frac{1}{2}$ tablespoon apple cider vinegar	

Roughly grind the mustard seeds in a spice grinder. If you like a smooth mustard, grind your seeds to a smooth powder. If you prefer a grainy mustard, stop grinding when the seeds still have a coarse texture. Transfer the ground seeds to a small bowl.

Stir in the water and let the mixture sit for about 10 minutes. Then add the vinegar, honey, and salt and combine well.

Transfer the mustard to a container with a tight-fitting lid. At this point it will be thin and somewhat bitter. The mustard will thicken and the bitterness will recede over the next several hours; by the next day, you'll have a lovely homemade condiment. For a thinner mustard, add more vinegar, water, or honey. For a thicker mustard, add a little flour.

ALMOND EXTRACT

Let's get the safety conversation out of the way first. All stone fruit kernels (and apple seeds) contain amygdalin, which, when combined with an enzyme in the human digestive system, produces cyanide. Now, we've all swallowed a few apple seeds, but the amygdalin is safely contained inside the skin of the seed, so unless you chewed up those seeds, you're fine. But this recipe specifically requires you to get inside the seed, so how can you enjoy this flavor and feel safe at the same time?

First, this is an extract. You will only be using small amounts of it. You will not be consuming the seed itself, and as I've said before, it's all about the dosage. The human body can detoxify small amounts of cyanide, and I believe that using small amounts of the extract is perfectly safe. But if that's not enough for you, try this.

Amygdalin is not heat-stable, so roast the kernels at 300°F for 10 minutes to make them safe. The resulting extract will be brown rather than clear, but the flavor is excellent. I'd read that roasting changes the flavor, but I've tried both methods, and while the flavors are slightly different, both are delicious.

YIELD: 1 CUP

> ¼ cup apricot pits
>
> 1 cup vodka

Crack open each apricot pit with a hammer. It's a tedious process, but worth the work.

Combine the kernels and vodka in a jar with a tight-fitting lid, cover the jar, and let it sit for 3 months.

After 3 months, strain off the liquid and bottle it to use as an extract, or, if you find the flavor as alluring as I do, take it a step further and turn your extract into noyaux, an almond-flavored liqueur. Store-bought noyaux is extremely sweet and often has a bright pink color that does not exist in nature. I make a less sweet, more delicious noyaux by adding simple syrup to my homemade almond extract. Add a little at a time until you're satisfied with the sweetness level.

NOCINO

Most people consider *nocino* to be a traditional Italian digestif, but the recipe actually originated in Britain. The Picts (a Celtic tribe from Scotland) harvested green walnuts at the summer solstice and celebrated the harvest by drinking the previous year's brew. Legend has it that the Romans took the recipe for *nocino* back to Italy when they left Britain behind.

You can make *nocino* with any kind of walnut as long as it's not ripe. The important thing is not what kind of walnut you use, but that the walnuts are young enough not to have developed a hard shell beneath the green husk. You should be able to slice through them with a sharp knife. Depending on where you live, the walnuts will be at the right stage in May, June, or early July.

Traditional *nocino* is spiced with cinnamon, vanilla, star anise, and cloves, but I prefer a combination of wild spices. Feel free to experiment with what grows near you.

Nocino can be served plain, over ice, in a cocktail, or (wait for it) poured over ice cream. This recipe makes approximately 1 gallon, but the recipe is easily scaled down if you have a small walnut harvest.

YIELD: 1 GALLON

2 pounds unripe walnuts, quartered	1½ teaspoons chopped sassafras root
½ cup dried sumac berries	
½ cup chopped spruce tips	1 tablespoon dried sweet clover
3 tablespoons crushed spicebush berries	2 to 3 quarts Everclear 151
	Simple syrup

Put the quartered nuts and spices in a 1-gallon jar and stir to combine. Cover with the Everclear, place the lid on the jar, and give it a good shake. Let the alcohol infuse for 40 days in a cool, dark place. The liquid will quickly change from clear to almost black.

After 40 days, strain off the solids and throw them away. Measure the liquid and combine with an equal amount of simple syrup. Let this combination sit for 90 days in a sealed container.

Strain the liquid through a fine coffee filter and pour into bottles. The *nocino* is ready to drink now, but its flavor will improve over the next 6 months.

CRETAN CHESTNUT STEW

While chestnuts are true nuts, their nutritional profile is closer to that of grains, and many cultures treat chestnuts as a carbohydrate-rich vegetable. On Crete, chestnuts are often served with potatoes and onions in a light coating of tomato sauce. If you have a favorite tomato sauce recipe, by all means, use it. If not, try mine, which is a variation on Marcella Hazan's much-loved, incredibly simple tomato sauce. The important thing is that the chestnuts are just coated in the sauce, rather than swimming in a bowl of it.

This recipe works best with fresh chestnuts. You can make it with rehydrated chestnuts, but the texture of the rehydrated nuts will always be a little too crunchy for my taste. I prefer them meltingly soft.

YIELD: 4 (1/2-CUP) SERVINGS

2 cups chopped tomatoes (with juice)

5 tablespoons butter

1 onion, peeled and halved

1/4 teaspoon salt

2 cups peeled chestnuts

Red wine or lemon juice

In a saucepan, combine the tomatoes, butter, onion, and salt. Bring the mixture to a simmer over medium heat, then reduce the heat to where it barely keeps the tomatoes bubbling. Cook, uncovered, for 45 minutes.

The original recipe asks you to throw away the onion before serving the sauce, but I can never bring myself to do that. The onions are delicious, and after 45 minutes in the pan, they have softened and fallen apart into bite-sized pieces. That's just what you want for this recipe.

Add the chestnuts to the tomato sauce and simmer, uncovered, for abut 30 minutes. Test a chestnut and see if the texture is to your liking—simmer longer if you'd like softer chestnuts. If you like wine, stir in a splash just before serving. Lemon juice also works well. The idea is to give the dish a bright dash of acidity to balance the richness of the chestnuts. Start with a tablespoon and increase until the flavor pleases you.

Cretan Chestnut Stew can be served as a side dish or as a main course with a salad and good bread.

Jerusalem artichokes

TUBERS
AND ROOTS

· ·

In my experience, foraged tubers and roots are not
as interchangeable as many other wild plant parts,
like greens and nuts. That doesn't mean they're
not versatile and delicious, it just means they have
their own distinct flavors and textures. So, while
the master recipes in this chapter can be adapted
to accommodate several different plants, there's
more focus here on individual, specialty recipes.

Some of the roots and tubers in this chapter are perennial, meaning they regrow from the same root system every year. But many of them are biennial, which means the plant establishes its root system and a basal rosette of foliage in the first year. The second year it grows a flower stalk, blooms, sets seed, and dies. For both perennial and biennial roots and tubers, the best time to harvest is usually in early spring or late fall, when the top growth of the plant is either dormant or almost dormant. (Lotus root is a notable exception.) During the growing season, plants draw sustenance from their tubers and roots, so there will be less flavor and nutrition stored in their tissue. Look for the first green shoots of spring as your cue to dig, or wait until the leaves and stems begin to turn yellow and die back in fall.

The table below provides some quick terms to help you talk about tubers.

bulb	A bulb is modified stem tissue that stores nutrition for the plant to draw on. Onions, shallots, and garlic are delicious bulbs.
geophyte	Geophyte is a general term for several kinds of underground storage tissue, including bulbs, tubers, and rhizomes.
rhizome	A rhizome is modified stem tissue that runs horizontally underground from the bottom of a plant, often forming a colony, with roots growing down from the bottom of the rhizome and stems growing up from the top of the rhizome.
root	The roots of a plant grow underground, absorbing water and nutrients from the surrounding soil and sending them up through the plant's vascular tissue.
stolon	A stolon is modified stem tissue that runs horizontally along the ground from the bottom of the plant, often forming a colony, with roots growing down from the bottom of the stolon and stems growing up from the top of the stolon.
taproot	A taproot is a thick, fleshy, generally vertical root that stores water and nutrition. The most familiar taproot is probably the carrot.
tuber	A tuber is modified stem tissue that serves as a food reserve, sprouting new stems from buds that grow along its skin. Potatoes are popular edible tubers.

Preserving the Harvest

COLD STORAGE

All my life I've wanted to have a root cellar. I'm pretty sure that's not going to happen on my tiny suburban lot, but a gal can dream. Roots and tubers can easily be stored for months in cool temperatures. Most of us make do with the crisper drawer in our refrigerators, but imagine how much you could store in a cool, subterranean room.

Root cellars are generally dug deep enough to maintain a temperature of 32–40°F and a high humidity level of 85–95% year-round. We don't all have the land or ability to have a root cellar, but you can fake it for a few months with barrels or bins filled with roots and tubers, covered with a thick layer of soil. Keep the bin in a frost-free garage or crawl space where temperatures stay in the 32–40°F range.

Whether you have a real root cellar or a crisper drawer full of foraged tubers, don't wash your tubers or roots until you're ready to use them. You can knock off any giant clods of dirt, but a coating of soil helps keep the harvest fresher longer.

DEHYDRATION

A surprising number of roots and tubers can be dried. Dehydrated lotus, burdock, and Jerusalem artichokes make good flours, and dandelion roots can be dried and roasted to make a flavorful coffee-like beverage or used as the base for homemade foraged bitters.

Hopniss tubers

General Techniques

ROASTING

Roasting enhances and sweetens the flavor of many tubers. Toss your tubers in olive oil with a little salt and pepper, then roast in a

400°F oven until the tubers are easily pierceable with a fork. Try this technique with daylily tubers, Jerusalem artichokes, burdock, salsify, and evening primrose. Roast dandelion root until it's dry to make a coffee-colored beverage or to infuse cream-based desserts.

PURÉE

Many roots and tubers can be puréed, just as you'd purée a potato. Boil the tubers or roots until they are soft (easy to pierce with a fork), then drain them and either purée in a food processor, a food mill, or a potato ricer. This works well with Jerusalem artichokes, daylily tubers, evening primrose, poppy mallow, dandelion roots, Queen Anne's lace, salsify, and hopniss. Puréed tubers can be made into fritters, used as a layer in shepherd's pie, or turned into a buttery, creamy mash.

RAW

Some tubers and roots are edible raw, but most are not. Daylily tubers, salsify, young burdock roots, and Jerusalem artichokes can be sliced and served raw and crunchy. They also make excellent pickles. However, there are caveats to both of the above. While raw Jerusalem artichokes make a tasty, crisp addition to a salad or crudité platter, some people find them hard to digest. And by hard to digest, I mean they give you significant gas. Significant. Gas. Raw daylily tubers are also a nice salad addition when sliced, but some people are allergic to daylilies and raw daylily seems to cause more GI distress in those with allergies than cooked daylily.

FLOUR

Jerusalem artichokes, lotus root, and burdock root make tasty, gluten-free flours. After dehydrating the sliced tubers, save them in a tightly sealed container until you're ready to grind them into flour. You can do this in a spice grinder or the dry grains cannister of a good blender, like a Vitamix. Remember, gluten-free flours won't bind or rise like traditional flours, so you should only substitute them for a portion of the traditional flour called for in your recipe.

Seasonal Availability

All of these tubers (except lotus) can be harvested in winter in places where plants go dormant but the ground does not freeze.

	Spring	Summer	Fall	Winter
burdock (*Arctium lappa*)	X		X	X
cattail (*Typha* spp.)	X		X	X
dandelion (*Taraxacum* spp.)	X		X	X
daylily (*Hemerocallis fulva*)	X		X	X
evening primrose (*Oenothera* spp.)	X		X	X
hopniss (*Apios americana*)	X		X	X
lotus (*Nelumbo* spp.)		X		
poppy mallow (*Callirhoe involucrata*)	X		X	X
Queen Anne's lace (*Daucus carota*)	X		X	X
salsify (*Tragopogon* spp.)	X		X	X
sunchoke or Jerusalem artichoke (*Helianthus tuberosus*)	X		X	X

Burdock (*Arctium* spp.) is a common vegetable in Japan, where it's called *gobo*. A much-maligned weed in the United States, burdock is known for its giant leaves, sticky, Velcro-like flowers, and its huge, stubborn roots that are seemingly impossible to dig up except in very loose sand. Burdock is a biennial, and its roots are best harvested at the end of its first growing season or the very beginning of its second, while the plant is not in active growth.

In Japan, burdock is often served as *kinpira*: peeled, sliced into matchsticks, and braised in mirin, sake, and soy sauce. If the roots are harvested at the end of their first season, they may be tender enough that no peeling is necessary—just give them a good scrub. In spring of their second year, you may want to peel them. After washing the root, take a bite of the raw root and decide if the skin is too fibrous to be pleasant. A simple roast (sliced into coins, tossed in olive oil, salt, and pepper, and baked for 15–20 minutes at 400°F) makes a delicious side dish or snack and showcases burdock's nutty, earthy flavor. It can also be pickled or used in stir-fries and gratins.

Cattails (*Typha* spp.) are some of the best-known wild edibles, offering multiple edible plant parts. But this is the roots and tubers chapter, so we're focused on the geophytes. Cattails spread by rhizomes, which are generally found buried just a few inches below the muddy surface of the wet soil that cattails love. They can be harvested any time of year, but tender, immature rhizomes are the tastiest. Older rhizomes are rich in edible starch, but they require a lot of work to access that starch.

Dig into the soil around the base of the cattails with your fingers and feel for slim rhizomes. If they continue straight until they end (rather than turn up at the end), they are young enough to be tender. These can be eaten raw, added to soups and stews, or steamed or boiled and served with butter and maple syrup, as Leda Meredith taught me. Cattail rhizomes can be blanched and frozen if you plan to use them as starch, but for eating, they are best used fresh.

Dandelions (*Taraxacum* spp.) are perennial plants that are despised by lawn lovers and adored by foragers. Their roots can be used in multiple ways—one popular use is drying, roasting, and using them as a coffee substitute. While the color is dark, like coffee, the flavor is all its own. Roasted roots can also be powdered and used to flavor milkshakes, ice cream, and custards. Dried (but not roasted) roots make an excellent base for cocktail bitters.

Dandelion roots can also be cooked as a vegetable. Like many root vegetables, older specimens may have a woody core. You can easily remove the surrounding flesh with the tines of a fork and mash it to serve as a side. The flavor is mild and somewhat reminiscent of a potato.

If you're going to dry or roast your dandelion roots, scrub them well and cut them to size before drying. They become very difficult to chop once dried. If you're going to eat your dandelion roots as a vegetable, wash the roots, boil for 2–3 minutes, then dunk in cold water to loosen the skins, which should slip off easily. Then continue to cook according to your recipe.

The daylily (*Hemerocallis fulva*) is slightly controversial because a small percentage of people are allergic and experience stomach upset after eating any of it. I'm sorry for those people, because daylilies are one of my favorite edible plants, and the tubers are my favorite edible part. They can be pickled or roasted like baby potatoes. Daylily tubers can be harvested almost any time, but they will be plumper at the beginning and end of their growing season.

There are literally thousands of cultivars of daylilies, but the only one I recommend from personal experience is the well-known ditch lily. Another common daylily—the yellow *H. lilioasphodelus*—is reputed to be edible, but I have never eaten it. Please note that daylilies are not the same as true lilies. This is an important distinction, and it's your job, as the forager and cook, to know the difference!

Evening primrose (*Oenothera* spp.) root is often described as having a strong peppery flavor, resembling that of parsnip or turnip, but I disagree. I'm not fond of either of those vegetables, but I like the flavor of evening primrose. *O. biennis* is the most commonly eaten species, best harvested in fall of its first year or early spring of its second year before the tall stem begins to grow. I've harvested in both seasons and found the flavor to be mild and appealing, perhaps with the slightest hint of black pepper.

Some people say that eating the raw root creates an itchy feeling in the back of the throat, but since the texture of the raw root can be quite tough and fibrous, I see no reason to experiment with that. Evening primrose should be peeled before eating. It can then be sliced and boiled, roasted, or mashed, making an excellent addition to soups and stews or served as a vegetable.

HOPNISS: IT'S DELICIOUS, BUT IS IT SAFE?

Hopniss used to be one of my favorite wild foods. But there's a potential problem with hopniss: it can make you sick. You won't die, but you will worship at the porcelain goddess for an hour or two. I'd read about this, but having no food allergies, I wasn't concerned. Then, after eating hopniss multiple times with no adverse effects, I became violently ill after a breakfast of hash browned hopniss. Apparently this is common among people who have the allergic reaction: You're fine with the tuber the first few times you eat it, then not at all.

Since this is not a common food, there is very little research being done. But we foragers are a close-knit community and we share information. Sam Thayer calculates the incidence of this reaction as occurring in about 5% of people who eat it, and that's a high incidence for food allergies. The cause is unknown, but there is speculation. Sam suggests that a long cooking time may be required to make the tuber reliably safe to eat. It's also possible that once you've had an allergic reaction to hopniss, you will always have that reaction.

I haven't been able to test that theory yet, because I no longer live where hopniss grows. But it's such a delicious wild food that I suspect I'll give it a try someday. Yes, the idea makes me nervous, but it's all in the name of research.

If after reading this you still want to try hopniss, cook it low and slow. First-year tubers have thin skins that don't require removal. Older tubers have thicker skins that you may want to peel, but it's not necessary; even the thicker skins aren't as thick as potato skins. The next time I find hopniss, I plan to cook them in my slow cooker for hours, just to be on the safe side. I'll let you know what happens.

Hopniss (*Apios americana*), or ground nut, is native to eastern North America and was a staple food for many native peoples. The flavor is wonderful—like a nutty potato. The tubers keep well in the refrigerator for months and can be harvested at any time of year. Hopniss is also a lovely plant to look at—it is a vine with highly fragrant blooms vaguely reminiscent of wisteria, a distant cousin.

Lotus root (*Nelumbo* spp.) is a traditional food in Asia, but it is generally ignored in the United States despite being a plentiful native plant. Many parts of both the sacred lotus (*N. nucifera*) and the native American lotus (*N. lutea*) are edible: the ripe nuts, young leaves, flower petals, and tubers. The tubers add flavor and beauty to any dish thanks to the intricate pattern of holes that run lengthwise through the root.

Lotus grows in water—you may have to dig down as far as a foot to reach the tubers, which grow linked together like a string of sausages. Cut between the linked tubers to remove what you want for cooking and leave the rest. Wash the lotus root, slice off each end, and look through the hollow tubes to make sure they're clean; if there's mud inside, rinse it out. Use a vegetable peeler to remove the skin.

No matter how you cook lotus, it will always retain a little bit of crunch. Deep-fry slices to make lotus chips or add fresh slices to stir-fries, soups, and stews.

Poppy mallow (*Callirhoe involucrate*), also known as winecup, is a perennial plant that grows in dry, sandy soils and produces numerous magenta flowers. It's a lovely plant, and is often grown as a garden ornamental by plant lovers who have no idea it's edible. In some climates, poppy mallow may go dormant in the heat of summer, but it will leaf out again in fall. This plant grows best in full sun and may take several years to develop a sizable taproot.

Poppy mallow taproots are mildly sweet, starchy, and slightly mucilaginous. Their texture, when cooked, is softer than that of a potato, but like a potato they offer something of a blank slate to which you can add all sorts of flavorings. The roots are best harvested from late fall, after the top growth has gone dormant, to early spring, before active growth begins in earnest. Poppy mallow roots can be stored for months in a root cellar. Slice them and add them to soups, stews, and stir-fries, or boil and mash them as a side dish. And plant a few in your garden while you're at it.

Queen Anne's lace (*Daucus carota*), sometimes called wild carrot, is indeed closely related to the cultivated carrot (*D. carota* ssp. *sativus*). Like other biennials, its taproots are best harvested between fall of its first year and spring of its second year. Any earlier and the root will be too small to be worth your time; any later and it will be tough and woody.

Second-year roots can be used to flavor soups and stews, but should be strained off the stock and discarded. Tender first-year roots can be washed and boiled or tossed in olive oil and roasted. Some first-year roots may have a thin, woody core, but the soft flesh—which is easily removed from the core with the tines of a fork—can be served as a buttered mash or puréed and used as a soup base. I have been known to nibble the boiled flesh of the Queen Anne's lace root like an ear of corn.

Salsify (*Tragopogon* spp.) is commonly called oyster root, but in my opinion, its flavor bears no resemblance to that of oyster. It's naturally sweet like a carrot, but with a milder flavor. Most wild salsify roots are very small, so you'll need to harvest a bunch if you're looking to make a side dish, but you can combine it with other roots and tubers in a mash, gratin, or soup. You can also wash, slice, and add raw roots to salads. Because the roots are so small and the skin is not usually thick, I recommend washing rather than peeling these taproots. Otherwise, you're left with nothing but a string.

The flower color may be yellow (*T. dubius*) or purple (*T. porrifolius*). Both are considered invasive in many states, so don't worry about overharvesting. Some salsifies are perennial, but the two species listed above are biennial, and you know what that means! Harvest the roots in late fall of their first season, or early spring of their second season.

Sunchokes (*Helianthus tuberosus*) are also known as Jerusalem artichokes. They're native to North America (not Jerusalem) and they are not closely related to artichokes, although they are in the same (very large) family. Sunchokes are perennial sun flowers and you may find their tubers for sale in farmers' markets. Cultivated sunchokes are round and lumpy and may grow to be as large as a baby's head. Wild sunchokes are smaller and generally long and narrow due to growing in leaner, tougher soils.

Now let's address the elephant in the room. Yes, it's true that Jerusalem artichokes are sometimes called Jerusalem fartichokes. The carbohydrate in sunchokes is inulin, which is not easily digested by the human digestive tract. As a result, it's one of the healthier carbs for diabetics because it is not easily broken down into sugars, but it can cause gas. Harvesting after the first frost and cooking thoroughly are believed to reduce gassiness this tuber can cause. I hope you won't let fear of flatulence keep you from enjoying this delicious food. Its flavor and versatility are truly remarkable.

ROASTED TUBER/ROOT
SOUP

Roasting your tubers and roots brings out their natural sweetness (don't forget, these are storage organs and contain sugars and other nutrients for the plant). That doesn't mean this soup will be sweet, but it adds a bit of caramelized richness to the dish. This recipe works well with sunchokes, salsify, evening primrose, burdock, and dandelions.

YIELD: 4 SERVINGS

3 cups washed and chopped (1-inch pieces) tubers or roots

1 medium yellow onion, peeled and cut into 1-inch chunks

Olive oil

Salt and pepper

2 cups chicken or vegetable stock

½ cup cream

Sage or chives, for garnish

Preheat the oven to 375°F.

If you're using sunchokes or salsify, there's no need to peel the tubers or roots—just give them a good scrub. The same goes for burdock if the roots are young and perfectly tender. If you use dandelions, skin them (see page 179). Evening primrose root should be peeled before cooking, as should burdock roots that aren't perfectly tender.

Toss the tubers or roots and onion in a drizzle of olive oil with a pinch of salt and pepper, then spread them on a baking sheet and roast for approximately 20 minutes. You want the onions to sweeten and brown, not to turn crispy and black. Remove the roasted vegetables from the oven and transfer them to a saucepan.

Add the stock to the roasted vegetables and bring to a boil. Cover and reduce the heat to a high simmer, cooking until the tubers are easily mashed with a fork. This should take 5–10 minutes. If you're using dandelions, look for pieces of woody core in the center of the roots and remove them before puréeing the mixture.

Allow the mixture to cool, then purée with an immersion blender, food processor, or blender. Return the purée to the saucepan and stir in the cream and ¼ teaspoon of salt. Reheat the soup, but do not let it boil.

Serve immediately with a grind of fresh pepper and sage or chives. Because these are fall harvests, I like to pair them with sage, an herb that tastes like autumn with its rich, warm flavors.

MASH

This is a simple yet worthy way to serve foraged geophytes. You can even combine odds and ends of different roots and tubers to create a blended mash. This recipe works well with sunchokes, salsify, evening primrose, dandelion, burdock, Queen Anne's lace, and hopniss. If you decide to use hopniss, please note the special instructions at the end of this recipe.

YIELD: 2 CUPS

3 cups washed and chopped (1–2-inch pieces) tubers or roots

1/2 onion, roughly chopped

Olive oil

1 tablespoon butter

1/4 cup plain Greek yogurt

1 teaspoon salt

1/2 teaspoon pepper

Boil the tubers or roots until they are easily pierceable with a fork. This should take 15–25 minutes, depending on their size. If you're using dandelions or Queen Anne's lace roots, remove the woody core from the boiled tubers before puréeing.

While the tubers or roots are boiling, sauté the onion in olive oil over medium heat until lightly caramelized.

Transfer the onion and tubers to a food processor and purée. Add the butter, yogurt, salt, and pepper, and purée some more. Taste and adjust seasoning if needed.

That's it. Ridiculously easy, right? This simple preparation lets the flavor of the roots and tubers shine. Snip a few scallions, sprinkle them on top of the purée to pretty it up, and serve it hot. Leftovers reheat like a dream.

NOTE: Sunchokes, salsify, and Queen Anne's lace do not require peeling, but evening primrose, dandelion roots, and older burdock roots should be washed and peeled before chopping.

If you're making this with hopniss, you'll want to cook it low and slow for safety's sake. Instead of boiling the chopped tubers until tender, put them in a slow cooker with enough water to cover them by several inches, turn the heat on low, and check back in 3–4 hours. Then proceed with the recipe.

PICKLES

Making refrigerator pickles is a great way to maintain the crunch of roots and tubers. While I often think pickle brine obscures the flavor of ingredients, many tubers have a mild flavor, so the pickling brine adds interest and spice. This recipe is recommended for daylily tubers, salsify, Jerusalem artichokes, burdock root (if it's young and tender), and cattail rhizomes.

Safe pickling depends on specific ratios of vinegar, water, and salt, so keep those proportions the same if you scale this recipe. Be sure to use kosher or canning salt. Table salt will give you a cloudy brine.

You may use either white or apple cider vinegar, as long as it has 5% acidity (the usual acidity level for commercial vinegars). You may increase the amount of vinegar in your brine if you prefer that flavor, but do not decrease the proportion of vinegar by adding more water.

Serve these as a crunchy side dish at a summer picnic or slice them up and add them to salads. They also work as an accompaniment to chicken or pork. This recipe can be easily scaled up to accommodate a bountiful tuber harvest.

YIELD: 1 CUP

1/2 cup water	6 whole, dried spicebush berries
1/2 cup vinegar	1 bay leaf
1 tablespoon kosher salt	1 cup cleaned and chopped
1/2 tablespoon sugar	(pickle-sized pieces) tubers or roots
	(Daylilies do not require chopping.)

Combine the water, vinegar, salt, and sugar in a saucepan and bring the liquid to a boil, whisking to dissolve the sugar and salt. Let the brine simmer for 2–3 minutes, then remove it from the heat and allow it to cool.

While the brine cools, add the spices to a half-pint canning jar, then add the prepared tubers or roots. Top with the cooled brine and let the pickles sit, refrigerated, for 48 hours. You could taste them after 24, but the flavors will meld better with a little more time in the fridge.

SKORTHALIA

My *yiayia* served traditional *skorthalia* (made with potatoes) as a dip, scooping it out onto pieces of pita bread. I prefer using celery sticks, cucumber slices, or fresh pepper slices as my delivery vehicle, so the crisp vegetable balances the creamy, carby, and very garlicky dip. And of course I make my skorthalia with foraged tubers and roots, like sunchokes, daylilies, salsify, and burdock.

If you have fresh field garlic or ramp bulbs, use those. But if you're making this dish in the fall, chances are you've preserved your foraged alliums by drying. Using powdered garlic is less authentic, but still very tasty. Grind up in a few dried allium leaves to add an interesting green color to the purée.

Back in the old days (and this dish dates back to ancient times), the ingredients were pounded by hand with a mortar and pestle. Some cooks still do it this way, claiming a food processor doesn't deliver the right consistency. I am not one of those cooks— have you met the food processor? It's one of my very best friends.

YIELD: 1½ CUPS

1 pound foraged tubers or roots	½ teaspoon pepper
7 to 8 field garlic or ramps bulbs (or 7 to 8 teaspoons dried field garlic/ramps powder)	¼ cup olive oil
	¼ cup lemon juice or white wine vinegar
1 teaspoon salt	¼ cup reserved water

Clean and chop the tubers or roots into 1-inch cubes, then boil them until they're easy to pierce with a fork. This will take 15–25 minutes, depending on the geophyte. Strain off the tubers or roots and set them aside to cool to room temperature. Reserve the cooking water.

In a food processor (hello, friend!), combine the garlic, cooked tubers, salt, pepper, olive oil, and lemon juice. Process until everything becomes a paste, adding up to ¼ cup of the reserved water if you need to thin the skorthalia.

Traditionally served at room temperature, skorthalia makes a great appetizer or side dish. While it may taste as creamy as mashed potatoes, it contains no cream or butter, making it a heart-healthy choice.

GRATIN

Gratins are a loose category of dishes. They usually include either cream or a béchamel sauce, and sometimes they include breadcrumbs or cheese (or both). I vary my ingredients depending on the flavor of the foraged tuber or root. For example, when I make a burdock gratin, I don't use cheese because I want to focus on the nutty, delicious flavor of burdock root. On the other hand, Jerusalem artichokes have a very mild flavor and benefit from the addition of a flavorful cheese. Bearing that in mind, this recipe works well with burdock, sunchokes, and evening primrose.

YIELD: 2 SERVINGS

1 cup cleaned, thinly sliced tubers

2 teaspoons butter

2 teaspoons flour

$^2/_3$ cup half-and-half or cream

1 teaspoon salt

$^1/_2$ teaspoon pepper

$^1/_2$ cup grated cheese (optional)

$^1/_4$ cup chopped mushrooms (optional)

If you have a mandoline, use it! Thin, uniform slices will cook and soften well in the oven when bathed in a rich cream sauce. If the roots are too small for a mandoline (like narrow burdock and evening primrose roots), slice them as evenly as possible by hand.

Preheat the oven to 375°F.

In a small saucepan, melt the butter and add the flour, whisking to create a smooth paste. Add the half-and-half, salt, and pepper and cook over medium heat to thicken. This will take at least 5 minutes, but don't rely on a clock alone. The sauce is done when it coats a spoon and does not taste like raw flour. Dip a spoon in the sauce and draw your finger across the back of the spoon. If the sauce closes up after your finger, it's not done. If your finger leaves a trail through the sauce, taste it to be sure it no longer tastes like raw flour.

Butter 2 ramekins or a small baking dish (enough to hold 2 cups) and lay down a layer of sliced tubers or roots. If you're using cheese or mushrooms, add a layer on top. Alternate layers of tubers/roots and flavorings until all the ingredients are used up. If you're using cheese, you'll want that to be the final layer so it browns up nicely. If you're using mushrooms, I suggest having the top layer be the tuber or root so the mushrooms don't dry out. Pour the cream sauce over the assembled gratin to within ½ inch of the top of the dish and bake for 45 minutes.

You can add breadcrumbs to the top of the gratin if you crave a crunchy crust. If you do, dot the breadcrumbs with butter before baking.

FRITTERS

This recipe works well with sunchokes, burdock, evening primrose, and daylily tubers. You *could* make it with lotus root, but that would be a waste of its physical beauty. Evening primrose and older burdock roots should be peeled before cooking. But sunchokes, daylilies, and young burdock root don't require peeling unless you have a personal aversion to the outer skin. Wash them well.

YIELD: 8 TO 10 FRITTERS

1 cup scrubbed or peeled, chopped tubers or roots

1 egg

1 tablespoon minced field garlic or 1 teaspoon dried field garlic powder

2 tablespoons mushroom powder

5 tablespoons breadcrumbs

3 tablespoons grated Parmesan or Romano cheese

Olive oil

Cut the tubers or roots into chunks no more than 1½ inches in size. (You will not need to chop daylily tubers.) Put the tubers in a saucepan, cover them with water, and bring to a boil. Let them simmer for 15 minutes or until you can easily pierce one with the tines of a fork. Burdock and evening primrose will take longer than sunchokes and daylily tubers.

Move the cooked tubers to a bowl and let them cool. (This is important because adding egg to hot tubers and roots will give you bits of cooked egg in the fritters.) Lightly mash the cooled roots or tubers; it's fine to leave it a little chunky.

Lightly beat the egg and add the field garlic, mushroom powder, breadcrumbs, and cheese. Gently incorporate the mash into the egg. If it's too loose to form into patties, add a few more breadcrumbs and a little more cheese. Mold the batter into small patties, 2–3 inches in diameter, and set aside.

Heat the oil in a frying pan over medium-high heat. The oil should sizzle immediately when you drip batter in the oil. If it doesn't, wait a little longer before starting the next one.

Cook the patties for about 3 minutes on each side. After flipping the fritters, press down on each one with the spatula to flatten it slightly. Remove them from the oil when they're golden brown and place them on a paper towel, which will absorb some of the oil.

These fritters are delicious served warm with a little hot sauce. Now that I think of it, a fried egg on top of one of these babies would make a pretty tasty breakfast.

DEEP-FRIED LOTUS ROOT

WITH SUMAC AND FIELD GARLIC

This is an exceptionally easy and pretty side dish. This tuber has excellent flavor and texture and is absolutely worth wading into the Mississippi up to your neck to forage for. Foraged lotus tubers are generally slimmer than store-bought tubers. I tell you this to manage your expectations.

YIELD: 2 SERVINGS

2 large or 4 small lotus tubers

Olive oil

2 tablespoons ground sumac powder

1 tablespoon ground field garlic

Wash and peel the lotus tubers, then cut them into slices approximately ¼ inch thick. Toss them in a bowl with a few tablespoons of olive oil, the sumac powder, and the garlic powder until evenly coated.

Pour ¼–½ inch of olive oil into a sauté pan and cook the lotus root over medium heat for about 3 minutes on one side. Flip each slice and continue to cook for another 3 minutes. Serve hot.

SUNCHOKE CAKE

Jerusalem artichokes have an aggressive growth habit (that may be the understatement of the year), so I've found myself needing to get creative with more than one enormous harvest. This cake recipe began as a twist on a classic carrot cake. It's now one of my favorite foraged desserts.

Like carrots, sunchokes are sweet, dense, and moist. This cake is tasty with a classic cream cheese frosting, but my favorite topping is a simple brown sugar icing with a sprinkle of foraged nuts. You could also make this with Queen Anne's lace, but since those tubers tend to be very small, it would be quite labor intensive.

I frequently make this as multiple small cakes and freeze some, unfrosted, to pull out when I need a quick dessert.

YIELD: 1 (9 X 13-INCH) PAN, 2 (8-INCH) ROUNDS, OR 6 (4-INCH) ROUNDS

FOR THE CAKE
$3/4$ cup butter, softened

1 cup sugar

6 eggs

$2^{1}/_{2}$ cups all-purpose flour

$^{1}/_{2}$ teaspoon salt

1 tablespoon baking soda

1 tablespoon dried, ground spicebush berries

$2^{1}/_{2}$ cups washed, grated Jerusalem artichokes

$^{1}/_{2}$ cup raisins (optional)

$^{1}/_{2}$ cup foraged nuts (optional)

FOR THE ICING
$1^{1}/_{2}$ cups brown sugar

5 tablespoons cream

2 teaspoons butter

$^{1}/_{8}$ teaspoon salt

$^{1}/_{2}$ teaspoon vanilla extract

Preheat the oven to 325°F.

In a bowl, cream together the butter and sugar. Add the eggs and combine well.

In a separate bowl, combine the flour, salt, baking soda, and spicebush berries. Mix well, then add to the egg mixture.

Add the grated sunchokes and the raisins and nuts if using them, then use a rubber spatula to fold all the ingredients together. By this time, the batter may be too heavy for an electric mixer. Because this batter is thick, this recipe works well in a springform pan. And by "works well," I mean it doesn't leak out the bottom all over your kitchen floor the way thinner cake batters do.

Pour the batter into a well-greased pan (or pans) and bake for 35 minutes or until a toothpick comes out clean from the center of the cake. Allow the cake to cool completely before frosting.

For the icing, combine the sugar, cream, butter, and salt in a small pan and bring just to a boil over medium heat, whisking constantly. Remove the pan from heat, stir in the vanilla, and let the icing cool long enough to reach a spreadable consistency. Spread the frosting over the top and sides of the cake, or pour the frosting on top and let it drip down the sides of the cake in glorious, sugary ribbons. Sprinkle a few more foraged nuts on top, if that's your jam.

The brown sugar doesn't dissolve completely and you'll feel the slight crunch of the sugar grain between your teeth. I think that's part of its charm, but if that doesn't appeal to you, go with a traditional cream cheese frosting.

ROASTED
DANDELION ROOT ICE CREAM

There's something about using a bitter flavor in a sweet dish that I just love. Most people use dandelion roots as a coffee substitute, which is a great way to go. But think about infusing that flavor in cream and turning it into panna cotta or ice cream. You might even add a handful of wild nuts or chocolate chips to give yourself some textural contrast.

YIELD: 3 CUPS

½ cup cleaned and chopped dandelion root

1 cup heavy cream

½ cup whole milk

A pinch of salt

⅓ cup sugar

2 egg yolks

½ teaspoon vanilla extract

Chocolate chips (optional—but are they?)

In a 250°F oven, roast the chopped, dried dandelion roots until they turn dark brown, like coffee beans. Depending on how finely you've chopped the roots, this may take 1½–4 hours. Grind the roasted roots in a coffee bean grinder—½ cup of chopped, roasted dandelion roots should give you about ¼ cup of powder.

Heat the cream, milk, salt, and sugar in a saucepan, whisking to dissolve the sugar. When the sugar is fully dissolved, add the dandelion powder and whisk to combine. Allow the liquid to just begin to simmer, then remove it from the heat, cover, and let the mixture steep for 30 minutes.

Strain the cream and discard the solids. You'll need to press the solids against the strainer to extract all the liquid possible; you should end up with just over a cup of infused cream.

Reheat the cream just to the simmering point. While the cream is heating, whisk the egg yolks together, then slowly add about ⅓ of the cream to the eggs, whisking constantly to integrate the two liquids without forming lumps of cooked egg. When the liquids are smoothly integrated, add them back into the remainder of the cream. Cook over medium-low heat until the liquid has thickened enough to coat the back of a spoon. Personally, I always have a hard time with this, because egg-based ice cream mixtures seem to coat the spoon from the very beginning. So I use a candy thermometer: when it reaches 170°F, the cream can come off the stove.

Strain the cream, add the vanilla, and allow the mixture to cool to room temperature. Refrigerate for at least 4 hours or overnight.

Churn the chilled cream in your ice cream maker, and if you'd like a little textural contrast in there, add a few chocolate chips or foraged nuts during the last 5 minutes of churning. The sweetness of the chocolate is a nice counterpoint to the bitterness of the roasted dandelion root. A little whipped cream would not go amiss.

POPPY MALLOW
HUMMUS

This recipe came to me from Julie Gracie, who also generously mailed me a box of taproots when my travel was limited due to the pandemic. In this recipe, the taproots replace the chickpeas used in traditional hummus, and the result is lighter and even tastier than the original. I've made a few small changes to Julie's recipe, but the inspiration is all hers!

Remember that almost any time you harvest a root crop, you're essentially killing the plant. Rhizomes can be harvested carefully, leaving most of the plant's root system intact, but when you harvest a taproot, that's it. Poppy mallow is often very abundant, but please keep sustainability in mind when you harvest.

YIELD: 1 CUP

10 peeled and chopped poppy mallow tubers (about 1⅓ cups)

2 tablespoons lemon juice

2 teaspoons minced field garlic or 1 teaspoon field garlic powder

2 tablespoons tahini

1 teaspoon salt

½ teaspoon pepper

1 tablespoon olive oil

1 tablespoon ground sumac powder

Peel the poppy mallow tubers, cut them into rough chunks, and boil them until they are soft and easy to pierce with a fork. Drain and set aside.

In a food processor or blender, combine all the ingredients except the sumac powder and blend for 4–5 minutes or until the mixture is very smooth. Add water by the tablespoon if the consistency feels too thick. You're aiming for the texture of traditional hummus.

Transfer the hummus to a bowl and sprinkle with the ground sumac powder for added flavor and color. Or, if you prefer green to red, sprinkle the hummus with dried ramp leaf powder or ground bee balm.

Skorthalia (page 188) and Poppy Mallow Hummus

Dried mushroom mix

MUSHROOMS

. . . .

Mushrooms are like the popular kids in high school.
You find them fascinating, but also a little scary.
They're mysterious, alluring, unpredictable, exciting,
and possibly dangerous. They make you nervous, but
you can't stop thinking about them. And if you treat
them carelessly, they'll never sign your yearbook.

Mushroom identification is *much* trickier than plant identification, often requiring a microscope and chemicals to distinguish among species. Identifying to the genus is simpler to do with the naked eye. And fortunately, there are plenty of delicious, easy-to-identify fungi with no poisonous look-alikes, so let's start with those. Come on, you know you want to hang with the cool kids.

Fungi can be categorized in many ways: toxic or nontoxic, toadstool or bracket fungus, ringed or not ringed, stemmed or stemless. But the first thing I look at is whether the mushroom is gilled or not gilled. It's easy to make this distinction quickly in the field, and it's especially nice to know the difference if you're a beginner. Why? Because there are no non-gilled mushrooms that will kill you. There are some that taste terrible and some that will make you sick to your stomach, but for those of you who are nervous but tempted by mushrooms, non-gilled mushrooms are a great place to start.

Mushroom Vocabulary

If you decide to become a mycophile, you'll inevitably build a library around the subject. There is much to be learned, and this book is neither a field guide nor an exhaustive mushroom reference. But since mushrooms have their own vocabulary, it's important to be able to talk the talk. Here are a few helpful terms to get you started.

bracket fungus	a stemless fungus that attaches directly to wood like a shelf
cap	the top of a mushroom
gills/lamellae	linear ridges of tissue on the underside of a mushroom cap that contain the spores
mushroom/ toadstool	the above-ground fruiting body of the fungus
mycelium	the underground network of tissue that produces a mushroom, comparable to the root system of a plant

pores	tissue on the underside of a mushroom cap that is perforated by tubes (pores), which contain the spores
puffballs	round, stemless mushrooms
ring/annulus	a circle of tissue on the upper stem of a mushroom that marks where a veil originally covered the developing mushroom
spores	single-celled, reproductive units of fungi, comparable to the seeds of plants
stalk/stipe	the stem of a mushroom
teeth	spore-producing spines of tissue found on the underside of a mushroom cap or arranged on the exterior of some capless mushrooms

In addition to the vocabulary, mushrooms have their own rules. If you want to play safely in the world of wild fungi, you need to know them.

1. Never eat a mushroom you can't identify with 100% certainty. This rule is important for all wild edibles, but mushrooms can kill you. They don't do it on purpose; it's in their DNA. I've passed up a few delicacies when I wasn't absolutely sure my identification was correct. Sure, I was disappointed when I got home, checked my field guide, and realized what I'd left behind. But better alive and disappointed than dead with a full stomach.

2. Start with non-gilled mushrooms. None will do permanent damage. It's still important to know *which* non-gilled mushrooms you've found, so this doesn't mean you can skip the ID process.

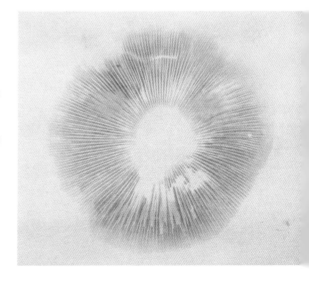

3. Make a spore print. Many mushrooms look similar on the outside, but their spores may tell a different story. Spores are held in the pore tubes of pored mushrooms and among the gills and teeth of gilled/toothed mushrooms. To make a spore print,

detach a fresh cap from its stalk, then cut the cap in half. Place one piece on a light sheet of paper, and the other on a dark sheet. Cover each with a drinking glass and let it sit overnight. In the morning, remove the glasses, lift the caps, and check the paper for a dusting of spores. Dark spores will show up better on light paper, and light-colored spores will be easier to see on dark paper. Spore color is an essential identification factor for many mushrooms.

4. Wash your mushrooms. We've all heard warnings about how washing mushrooms will turn them soggy or rob them of their flavor, but this simply isn't true. Washing your mushrooms is a much easier and better way to clean them than dry brushing. You can even soak them briefly to flush out spiders and insects. Mushrooms actually absorb very little water in the cleaning process, and what they do absorb will quickly be released by either dehydrating or cooking. If you don't believe me, ask Harold McGee, Alton Brown, or Jacques Pépin. Or prove it to yourself with a simple experiment: weigh your harvest, wash it, let it air dry, and weigh it again. I'll wait.

5. Cook your mushrooms. Yes, I've seen raw button mushrooms sliced into salads, but the people who make those salads are not necessarily mushroom experts. The cell walls of mushrooms are made of chitin,[1] not cellulose.[2] Humans do not digest chitin well—in fact, we may not be able to digest it at all. Scientists disagree. Cooking breaks down chitin, making mushrooms easier for us to digest. Cooking also makes the nutrients in mushrooms more accessible to the human body. And finally, cooking kills any insects or spiders that may have hitchhiked back to your kitchen on your mushroom harvest. I'm not saying that an edible mushroom will make you sick if you eat it raw, and I've personally enjoyed a few raw slices of delicious matsutake mushrooms. But in general, cooking your mushrooms will help you avoid stomach upset.

6. Join a local mushroom club. You may be surprised by how many fellow mycophiles there are in your area. The North American Mycological Association lists local clubs on its website.

The thrill of the mushroom hunt is real. If you want in on the action, buy yourself a few good field guides, take some classes, and go on every mushroom

---

1. Chitin is the primary component of cell walls in fungi, insects, crustaceans, fish scales, and bird beaks.
2. Cellulose is the primary component of the cell walls in plants and algae.

We don't say, "I'm going blueberry hunting." We call that "blueberry picking." And we don't say that we're going hunting for wild greens, we say that we're gathering greens. But mushrooms are different. A mushroom that comes up one year in a certain spot, may not be there next year, even if it's a perennial mushroom. Plants are dependable that way: the top growth dies back in winter and regrows from the roots. Not so with the fungus family. Mushrooms are very picky about their growing conditions and require precise combinations of moisture, temperature, and soil type. Some even have mycorrhizal[3] relationships with certain plants and will only grow where their mycelium can intertwine with those plants' root systems. Which means that, just like the hunter who goes out for deer or wild turkey, the forager who goes out for mushrooms may or may not come home with the hoped-for harvest. This unpredictability and uncertainty makes a successful harvest something to celebrate, with whoops of joy and your own special happy dance. The risk of coming home empty-handed is much greater with mushrooms than it is with plants, but the triumph of a good mushroom hunt is something every forager remembers.

---

3. A mycorrhizal relationship is a mutually beneficial relationship between a fungus and the roots of a plant, where the mushroom acts as an extension of the plant's root system, allowing it to absorb more nutrients, and the plant provides nutrients to the mushroom.

walk you can find. Make spore prints and join a local club. Knowledge is power and mushrooms are delicious.

Special Equipment

Mushroom hunting is pretty low tech, but there are a few things that will make your hunt easier and more productive.

Foragers are divided on the best way to harvest mushrooms. Some people cut them off at soil level, and others dig down and lift the mushroom up from its base. Because certain identification characteristics are located below the soil,

I use my bare fingers to dig under the base of the mushroom and gently lift it up, preserving as much of the base as possible.

Still, I carry a mushroom knife for several reasons. The brush is useful for gently cleaning soil from the gills and stems. The curved blade lets you carve off the soil-covered layer of stem that was below ground, preserving the clean, inner flesh. And the blade is sharp enough to cleanly separate a bracket fungus from tree bark without damaging either the tree or the fungus.

Small paper bags keep mushroom species separated in your backpack. Both paper and waxed paper allow the mushrooms to breathe; fungus in plastic bags may quickly turn to mush. In a pinch, you can roll your mushrooms in sheets of waxed paper or parchment paper, then twist the ends to hold them in place.

Leave the mushroom basket at home, unless you want to advertise to the world that you're in primo mushroom territory. Foragers guard their best spots, only sharing them with trusted friends. A backpack or pillow case will hide your harvest.

Preserving the Harvest

Mushrooms are highly perishable, and different mushrooms require different preservation methods to maintain their deliciousness. While some mushrooms will last a few days in the refrigerator, others will deliquesce[4] in a matter of hours. Don't linger when it comes time to preserve your mushroom harvest.

DEHYDRATION

Some mushrooms actually taste better dried than fresh. As with herbs, drying intensifies the flavor, because it removes the water, leaving the tasty bits behind. I didn't believe this until I ate my first fresh porcini (roasted in butter and miso), and my first dried porcini sauce in the same meal. Both were delicious, but the flavor of the dried mushrooms was more complex and intense.

Black trumpets and cinnabar chanterelles are delicate and dry quickly; they can be dehydrated whole. Porcinis, oysters, and morels should be cut into slices no more than ¼ inch thick, then dried in a single layer in a dehydrator at 125°F.

---

4. I just love this word. It's pronounced deh-lih-qwess and it means (basically) to liquify in front of your eyes. It's a common characteristic of the *Coprinus* mushrooms, i.e. the inky caps and shaggy manes.

If you live in a dry climate, you may air dry your mushrooms, but be sure to protect them from insects, animals, and snails by using the double-screen method (see page 17).

Depending on where you live, it may take anywhere from six to twelve hours for your mushrooms to dry in a dehydrator, and more than that if you're air drying. Stop when you can snap one in half with your fingers, and keep your dried mushrooms in sealed containers out of the light. Correctly dried and stored, your foraged mushrooms can last for years, although they'll taste best within the first year.

RAW FREEZING

Hen of the woods mushrooms (aka *maitake*) can be giant mushrooms. I wish you could see the photo of me lying on one of those blue tarps surrounded by hens. Good times. Fortunately, hens are among the easiest (and fastest) mushrooms to preserve. All you have to do is clean them and freeze them—no cooking required.

After cleaning, carve away the tough, woody center of the fungus and save it to make *duxelles* (page 206). Rinse off the tender parts of the mushroom and spread them out to dry in a single layer. Freeze them in Ziplock or vacuum-seal bags, and that's it!

I've experimented with drying hen of the woods, and while the flavor is nice, the texture isn't as good as frozen hens. If you don't have enough freezer space, dehydrating is a viable alternative, but don't expect a fresh mushroom texture upon rehydration. (They never fully soften.) Grind dry hens into a powder to use in soups and sauces.

SAUTÉ & FREEZE

This is the method that works best for the greatest number of mushroom species. Chicken of the woods, honey mushrooms, wine caps, and field mushrooms, among others, are best preserved by this two-step process. Butter and oil are both good choices; you'll want about two tablespoons of fat for each cup of mushrooms.

Think about how you'll use the mushrooms before you cut them for the frying pan. If you're going to use chicken of the woods as a chicken substitute, chop or tear your mushrooms into large pieces. Mushrooms destined for a sauce or pastry can be cut into smaller chunks.

Melt the butter (or warm the oil), and add the mushrooms. Cook them over medium heat until they've released all their liquid and the butter or oil has been absorbed. Remove the mushrooms from the heat and let them cool before freezing. Try freezing individual containers or Ziplock bags, each holding one cup of mushrooms. That makes it easy to thaw just the right quantity for your next recipe.

DRY SAUTÉ & FREEZE

Chanterelles are a special mushroom, best preserved in a special way: dry sautéed, then frozen. To dry sauté chanterelles, slice them into pieces about ¼ inch thick, then cook them in a hot, dry pan over medium-high heat. No oil, no butter, just heat.

Cook them until all the liquid has evaporated, stirring to prevent burning. This method gives chanterelles great texture and accentuates their flavor. Remove the cooked mushrooms from the heat, then let them cool before freezing them in measured quantities.

General Techniques

DUXELLES

When you've invested hours foraging for wild mushrooms, it's hard to give up even an ounce of your harvest. But not every mushroom you bring home is tender enough to eat as is. Let's say you hit the hen of the woods mother lode and you've already cooked with or preserved all the tender caps. The solid stem feels too dense and woody to use in large pieces, but it's fresh and smells great. What to do? *Duxelles* to the rescue!

Finely dice the leftover mushroom. For every pound of mushrooms, you'll need at least a tablespoon of diced allium. Onions and shallots are both good. Heat a heavy pan, add a few tablespoons of olive oil, then add the mushrooms and alliums and stir to coat. Add salt and pepper to taste (start with ½ teaspoon salt and ¼ teaspoon pepper) and ½ teaspoon dried bee balm. Cook over medium heat until all the liquid has evaporated and the mushrooms and alliums start to brown. Add ¼ cup white wine, and continue to cook until the liquid has all been absorbed. Remove the mushrooms from the heat and allow them to cool, then freeze in ½-cup portions.

Duxelles can be added to soups or stews for instant flavor, combined with cream for a fast sauce, or mixed with cheese for a pasta filling.

POWDER

There are times when you find a choice mushroom at a less than choice stage. Or maybe you dried a mushroom to preserve it and aren't satisfied with the texture after rehydration. Or maybe you've found a mushroom with a great flavor but a difficult texture, even when it's very young. This is when you should make mushroom powder. Mushroom powder adds umami complexity (see page 22) to savory dishes and it's easy to keep on hand.

I first experimented with mushroom powder when I found a tender, young black-staining polypore (*Meripilus sumstinei*). It was fibrous and tough no matter how I tried cooking it, but I could tell the flavor was wonderful. So I sliced the mushroom, dried the slices, and ground them into a fine powder using a spice grinder. The flavor is rich, almost chocolatey, and I use it in cream sauces, soups, casseroles, and molés.

Strongly flavored mushrooms work best for powder. Start with mushrooms that are best preserved by drying, like black trumpets and porcini. Hen and chicken of the woods also work well.

ROASTING

Roasted mushrooms make an excellent side dish, and this simple technique can be applied to every wild mushroom I've ever harvested—what changes is how long you roast them. Thick, meaty mushrooms (like hens, chickens, porcinis, and oysters) can take 30 minutes, while smaller, more delicate mushrooms (morels, black trumpets, cinnabar chanterelles) may only need 10–15 minutes in the oven.

Oil a shallow baking pan and preheat the oven to 400°F. In a bowl, toss the mushrooms with olive oil to coat. Season with garlic, salt, and pepper and spread the mushrooms in a single layer in the pan. Bake for 15 minutes for meaty mushrooms (or 5 minutes for delicate mushrooms), then check the pan for liquid. Pour off any excess (and save it, it's delicious!), then return the pan to the oven and finish up the roasting.

Likely the most common way to prepare mushrooms, sautéing gives you loads of flexibility regarding herbs, spices, and fats. If you're working with just-washed or rehydrated mushrooms, cook them first with no fat at all as a dry sauté. Once they've released all their liquid, add the fat, herbs, and spices. If you're going for an overall warm and tender mushroom, perhaps something to put on top of steak or chicken, keep them moving in the pan, allowing for just a hint of browning and crispness. If you're feeling bold and would like to encourage caramelization, let the mushrooms sit in the pan with the fat until they're well-browned and crisp on the bottom, then turn them and do the same for the other side. This technique works best with meaty, individual mushrooms or mushrooms cut into large chunks. You're not aiming for a mushroom chip, but something that combines a crispy outside and a soft inside.

Seasonal Availability

The first time I found bear's head tooth (*Hericium americanum*), I wasn't 100% sure what it was, so I left it on the tree. Boy, did I kick myself later. This is a choice mushroom with a smooth, delicate texture and a flavor that many compare to scallops. I think that's an accurate description of the texture, but to me the flavor is mildly mushroomy with a hint of sweetness. Lion's mane (*H. erinaceus*) has a similar texture and flavor, and both *Hericiums* are toothed mushrooms that grow on hardwood trees or fallen logs.

All toothed mushrooms are tricky to clean, because the delicate teeth break off easily. But *Hericiums* are usually pretty clean, since they don't grow on the ground. If you must rinse them off, give them a gentle swish in some lukewarm water and let them air dry. These mushrooms have a high water content, so try a dry sauté and then freeze to preserve them.

Black trumpets (*Craterellus cornucopioides*) are stealthy. They most often grow in conjunction with sphagnum moss near oak and beech trees, and since they're small, low-growing, and the color of soil, it's not easy to spot them until you're right on top of them. The first time I found black trumpets in our yard, I went inside to confirm my ID in several field guides. When I came back outside,

	Spring	Summer	Fall	Winter
bear's head tooth (*Hericium* spp.)			X	
black trumpets (*Craterellus cornucopioides*)		X	X	
boletes (*Boletus edulis* & others)		X	X	
chanterelles (*Cantharellus* spp.)		X	X	
chicken of the woods (*Laetiporus* spp.)		X	X	
field mushrooms, the prince, and horse mushrooms (*Agaricus* spp.)	X	X		
giant puffballs (*Calvatia gigantea*)		X	X	
hedgehogs (*Hydnum repandum*)		X	X	
hen of the woods (*Grifola frondosa*)			X	
honey mushrooms (*Armillaria* spp.)			X	
lobsters (*Hypomyces lactifluorum*)		X	X	
morels (*Morchella* spp.)	X			
oysters (*Pleurotus* spp.)	X	X	X	X
shaggy manes, ink caps (*Coprinus comatus, Coprinopsis atramentaria*)		X	X	
wine caps (*Stropharia rugosoannulata*)		X	X	

I couldn't find the mushrooms again, even though I knew exactly where to look!

The black trumpet has no poisonous look-alikes. Just a few will impart a strong and wonderful taste to any dish. This is a midsummer-to-early-fall mushroom and grows best in partial or full shade after some soaking rain. Because black trumpets usually grow in moss, they are among the cleaner mushrooms to harvest. Gently grip the bottom of the trumpet and pull; it will come right off in your hand, perhaps with a little bit of moss attached, but without the dirt that often accompanies mushroom gathering. They dry well and can be rehydrated with little, if any, loss of flavor.

The king of all boletes (literally) is *Boletus edulis*, also known as porcini, cep, penny bun, *Steinpilze*, and king bolete. It's one of the most delicious and sought-after edible mushrooms in existence. The king bolete is easy to identify by its brown to reddish-brown cap, its thick, cream-colored stem (often as wide as the cap itself), and the delicate white pattern of netting at the top of the stem. The flesh of the king bolete does not stain blue when cut.

The timing of porcini season depends on where you hunt. The two most prolific porcini-producing regions in the United Sates are the Rocky Mountains (late summer) and the Pacific Northwest (spring and fall). You'll often find porcini pushing up through layers of dried evergreen needles, creating "mush-humps," so watch where you walk. These boletes most often grow in conjunction with conifers like spruce, fir, and pine, and have a mycorrhizal relationship with these trees.

King boletes dry spectacularly well, and a full jar of dried porcini smells rich and complex—almost smoky. They rehydrate easily in warm water after a 20-minute soak. There are many different boletes, some tasty, some bitter, some causing stomach upset. But since none will kill you, boletes are a good place to start your wild mushroom exploration.

Am I the only person on the planet who doesn't think chanterelles (*Cantharellus* spp.) smell like apricots? Because really, I don't. I love them, they're delicious, but I don't get the fruity scent. Chanterelles are known for having what mycologists call false gills. This means that instead of true gills, they have folds underneath the cap that look like gills. Once you recognize the unique, vase-like shape of the chanterelle, you'll be forever searching the summer woods for them.

The smooth chanterelle and the golden chanterelle are good-sized, substantial mushrooms. The cinnabar chanterelle (with its gorgeous vermillion color) is quite a bit smaller, maxing out at 2 inches tall. You'll see dried chanterelles for sale, but their texture, when rehydrated, is never quite tender enough to suit me. Better to dry sauté and freeze to preserve.

Chicken of the woods (aka sulfur shelf) is the common name for both *Laetiporus sulphureus* (a fall mushroom) and *L. cincinnatus* (a summer mushroom). Both are bright orange, and the underside is either yellow (*L. sulphureus*) or white (*L. cincinnatus*). Chickens are large mushrooms, coming back year after year until they kill their host tree, then coming back every year for a few years after that until all the nutrients in the wood are exhausted. It's a polypore, which means it has pores, not gills.

Someone, somewhere, thought this mushroom tasted like chicken (hence its name), but I disagree. True, it's got a dense texture that can substitute for chicken in soups or casseroles, but the flavor is definitely fungal. Chicken of the woods gets tough as it ages, but you may be able to trim tender new growth from the outer edges of older brackets. To preserve your chickens, give them a rough chop, sauté them in butter or oil, then freeze. You can dry chicken mushrooms in a dehydrator, but they never become fully tender when rehydrated. I only do this if I'm going to powder the mushroom to use in soups or stews.

Field mushrooms (*Agaricus* spp.) include both edible and nonedible mushrooms, and identification within this genus is tricky, even for experts. If you've eaten a button mushroom from the super market, you've eaten an *Agaricus*. Among the tastiest species are *A. campestris* (the field mushroom), *A. augustus* (the prince), and *A. arvensis* (the horse mushroom). Visually, they resemble the white button mushroom, although they are larger and their gills are pink or brown. These are all choice, tender, mild mushrooms that are often found in vast quantities in a single location, so it's worth getting to know them.

Giant puffballs (*Calvatia gigantea*) can be truly giant—bigger than your head. The first time I saw one, I literally thought it was a soccer ball someone had left in a field. Puffballs are good if they are entirely white inside. If there's any yellow, green, or purple when you slice it open, they are too far gone. Leave them outside to release their spores and make more puffballs.

Pure white puffballs can be cut into slices and browned in butter or olive oil. They are delicious all on their own. You could also dip them in beaten egg and breadcrumbs and sauté them. To preserve puffballs for later use, either sauté and freeze the slices or dry them to use as a mild mushroom powder.

Hedgehog mushrooms (*Hydnum repandum*) have no poisonous look-alikes and are easy to identify. A quick look at the underside of the orange cap will clarify matters. These mushrooms are neither gilled nor pored. They have short, spiny teeth that hang down like mini-stalactites. Hedgehogs fruit from summer through mid-fall and are seldom bothered by insects. These mushrooms are tricky to clean because of their numerous, delicate teeth, so try to keep them clean from the start. Slice the stalk of the mushroom just above the ground, rather than pulling up the dirty stump. If you must wash them, swish them gently in a bowl of lukewarm water.

Hedgehogs have a delicate flavor with an edge of nuttiness and combine well with mild flavors like eggs or rice. Preserve them by sautéing and freezing.

If you've ever eaten *maitake* mushrooms, you've eaten hen of the woods (*Grifola frondosa*). This meaty bracket fungus is a polypore that grows at the base of hardwood trees or from underground tree roots; it has pores, not gills. It's not unusual for a large hen to weigh many pounds. Hen of the woods can be hard to spot because its color is somewhere between that of oak bark and brown oak leaves; you need sharp eyes for this treasure hunt.

Hen of the woods is a fall mushroom that appears after a good, soaking rain. I'm guessing it got its common name because someone thought it looked like the ruffled feathers of a hen, although that's a stretch. Numerous gray-brown caps or brackets (with white undersides) branch off of a thick, fibrous white stem. The brackets are the tender, choicest parts of the mushroom, but don't throw away that tough, fibrous stalk! It can be used to make mushroom stock or minced and made into *duxelles* (page 206).

Hen of the woods has no poisonous look-alikes, which makes it an excellent mushroom for beginning foragers. And, it's one of the few mushrooms that can be frozen without blanching or cooking. Clean it, cut it into pieces, then freeze. It's as simple as that.

Honey mushrooms are not for beginners. But they are so tasty and often so plentiful that you should definitely learn about them. There are two different species known as honey mushrooms: the ringless honey (*Armillaria tabescens*) and the ringed honey (*A. mellea*). Both grow at the base of hardwood trees or from roots. Because there are some poisonous look-alikes, be cautious with this mushroom. Be sure to take a spore print. Honeys give you a white spore print, unlike their several look-alikes that all have brownish spores.

Honey mushrooms grow in large, clumping clonal populations, so it's often easy to harvest vast quantities. They dry well. These mushrooms should be cooked at least 10 minutes, either sautéed or added to soups and stews. Some people only eat the caps and leave the stems in the field. What a waste. Firm, young stems are tender and tasty, and often very long, providing lots of mushroom mass. Use a vegetable peeler to get rid of the outer skin, then cook up those stems.

Ink caps (*Coprinopsis atramentaria*) and shaggy manes (*Coprinus comatus*) are closely related. There are two tricky things about these mushrooms. First of all, they deliquesce, and therefore must be used almost immediately. Second, some people have negative reactions when combining alcohol with ink caps. I'd read that eating ink caps within 48 hours of consuming alcohol would result in nausea and vomiting. Since I'm someone who enjoys a glass of wine with dinner, this was problematic, so I decided to put it to the test. When I first found ink caps, I'd had wine the night before. I knew the mushrooms wouldn't last long, so I took a chance and ate the mushrooms within 24 hours of consuming wine. I had no trouble at all and have repeated the experience several times since. So, is it an old wives' tale, conceived of by a teetotaling cookbook writer? I don't know. If you want to be 100% safe, wait 48 hours between consuming alcohol and eating ink caps. These mushrooms are best preserved by sautéing and freezing.

I have a love-hate relationship with lobster mushrooms (*Hypomyces lactifluorum*). I love them because they're big and meaty, easy to recognize, and the product of a very cool process. Lobster mushrooms are actually two fungi in one. Two different, edible (but not super delicious) mushroom species (*Lactarius piperatus* and *Russula brevipes*) are parasitized by the *H. lactifluorum* fungus, which turns the host mushrooms orange and gives them a scent highly reminiscent of shellfish.

And therein lies the problem. Lobster mushrooms may look and smell like lobster, but they have absolutely no lobster flavor. What a disappointment. If not for the hype of the name and the fragrance, I'd be perfectly happy to find such a substantial mushroom. But when you expect something to taste like lobster and it tastes like mushroom, well . . . do you see my point? Lobster mushrooms dry well. If you can forget about the "lobster" part, you'll enjoy the harvest.

Morels (*Morchella* spp.) are much beloved as the first mushrooms of spring in most places. There are several tasty species, including yellow morels, gray morels, and black morels. Generally, all of these grow best in warm, moist conditions, often close to dead or dying deciduous trees such as elms, cottonwoods, oaks, and ash, and in old apple orchards. On the West Coast, morels are often found close to Douglas fir and other conifers, and large flushes of gray morels (sometimes called the fire morel or burn morel) often follow forest fires.

Beginning morel hunters often fear the false morel. There are several species of mushrooms with this common name, but the most common is *Gyromitra esculenta*. This fear is unfounded, as it is *very* easy to tell the difference between false and true morels. True morels are hollow from head to toe. If you find what you think is a morel, slice it open lengthwise. If your mushroom is not hollow (both stem and cap) you do *not* have a true morel. True morels also have a distinctive cap; it is spongy and netted. False morels, on the other hand, look more like a brain on a stick instead of a net on a stick. While some people enjoy eating false morels, there are enough reports of gastrointestinal distress to make me cautious. I recommend sticking to true morels.

Oyster mushrooms (*Pleurotus* spp.) grow in clumps on dead and dying wood. Not only are they mild, tasty, versatile mushrooms, but they also have a longer harvest season than any mushroom I know. Oysters tolerate colder temperatures and are most abundant in fall and winter. Even after a frost or two, you can, after adequate rain, count on oyster mushrooms for your winter table. I've harvested frozen oyster mushrooms in the middle of winter, then thawed and cooked them with no discernible decline in tastiness. To preserve them for later, you can dry oyster mushrooms in a dehydrator or sauté them in butter or oil and freeze. Large, meaty oyster caps can be grilled, broiled, or fried like steaks with butter and garlic.

Wine caps (*Stropharia rugosoannulata*) give you two identification clues in their name. Young mushrooms have a red cap, like red wine, which fades with age. And *annulus* means ring, describing the pronounced ring of tissue around the upper part of the stem. They're sometimes called mulch mushrooms because they are so often found growing in mulched garden beds. In fact, the first time I found them was walking through the New York Botanical Garden on my way to (wait for it) a mushroom class! I saw one growing in a mulched perennial bed and picked it to bring to class. They were all over the grounds!

These are meaty mushrooms with excellent texture and flavor. And as a bonus, they're one of the easier mushrooms to cultivate in your backyard. Wine caps are best preserved by sautéing and freezing.

REHYDRATING MUSHROOMS

How do you gauge volume when you're rehydrating mushrooms? If a recipe calls for 2 cups of chopped mushrooms and you're working with rehydrated mushrooms . . . is there a formula? Sadly, no. But I can get you started:

Dried mushrooms absorb liquid, but different types of mushrooms absorb different amounts of liquid. Whatever mushroom you're using, the rehydrated version will have more volume than the dried version.

To complicate the matter even further, we usually dry mushrooms whole or in large slices, and most recipes call for mushrooms to be chopped. When mushrooms (or anything else, for that matter) are chopped, they take up less space in a measuring cup than larger slices do because less volume is lost to large air spaces between pieces. Whatever mushroom you're using, the chopped version will have less volume than the sliced version.

Does the increase in volume due to rehydration balance out the decrease in volume that results from chopping? No. Maybe. Sometimes. But you can't count on it. I suggest increasing the volume of the dried mushrooms by 25–50% to make sure you get enough rehydrated mushrooms for the recipe.

In other words, if a recipe calls for 2 cups of mushrooms (chopped), I'd start with 2½–3 cups of dried, sliced mushrooms to be sure I have enough for the recipe. You might have a few left over, but that's better than not having enough, right? You can always toss the leftovers into eggs, soup, or bread pudding.

ACORN & MUSHROOM
SOUP

This soup is filling, delicious, and, thanks to its low fat content, very healthy. Soup is an excellent way to use hot-leached acorns (page 152). Hot leaching is faster than cold leaching, but it cooks the starch, making the acorns less useful as flour. With soup, no starch is required for binding like it would be in a baked good.

YIELD: 4 SERVINGS

1 cup fresh or rehydrated mushrooms

1 carrot, peeled and chopped

1 celery stalk, chopped

1 medium onion, chopped

2 tablespoons butter or oil

1½ cups shelled, leached acorn pieces

⅓ cup sherry or white wine

2 bay leaves

4 cups chicken or mushroom stock

Salt

½ cup non-fat plain Greek yogurt

Parsley, chopped

To rehydrate the mushrooms, place them in a shallow bowl and add enough warm water to cover. When the mushrooms are soft (this may take 15–30 minutes), remove them from the water and chop them into large pieces. Save the leftover soaking water for later.

Sauté the carrot, celery, and onion in the butter until softened. Add the mushrooms and acorn pieces and stir to combine. Sauté for another few minutes.

Add the sherry, bay leaves, and stock, and simmer, covered, for 1 hour. Let the soup cool, then purée the mixture in a blender or with an immersion blender. Add salt to taste. Reheat the soup, and use additional stock or the leftover water from rehydrating the dried mushrooms to thin the mixture to your preferred consistency.

Remove the soup from the heat and stir in the yogurt, then top with chopped parsley and serve.

MUSHROOM-STUFFED
RAVIOLI

Packaged wonton wrappers simplify this recipe, but if homemade pasta is something you love to make, by all means, feel free. For me, the thin wanton wrappers provide the perfect ratio of noodle to filling.

YIELD: 30 TO 40 RAVIOLI

2 cups roughly chopped mushrooms

1 stick butter, divided

1 tablespoon olive oil

3 cloves garlic, thinly sliced

Salt and pepper, to taste

$1/4$ cup mushroom broth

$1^{1}/_2$ cups ricotta cheese

$3/8$ cups grated Parmesan cheese

12 sage leaves, finely chopped

If you rehydrate mushrooms for this recipe, save the soaking water and use that as the mushroom broth.

Combine the mushrooms, ½ stick butter, olive oil, and garlic, and cook over medium heat until softened. Add salt and pepper to taste, then add the mushroom broth. Cook over medium heat until the mixture cooks down and the liquid is mostly evaporated. Remove from the heat and let cool.

In a blender, combine the ricotta cheese with the grated Parmesan, then add the cooled mushroom mixture and blend until smooth. If the mixture is too thick, add a little more broth. Taste and adjust the spicing if necessary.

Place a teaspoon of mushroom filling in the center of a wonton wrapper, then brush the edges of the wrapper with water and fold the wrapper in half diagonally, pressing the edges together to form a triangle. Make as many raviolis as you have filling for (any extra can be frozen for later use) and allow the stuffed pasta to air dry for 1 hour. Boil briefly, until pasta is cooked through; this may only take 2 or 3 minutes. This is a delicate ravioli and will break apart if overstuffed or overcooked.

Melt the remaining butter over medium heat in a frying pan. When the butter has melted, add the sage and continue to heat until the butter turns brown and starts to smell nutty. Remove from the heat and set aside.

After draining the pasta, serve and top with the brown butter–sage sauce, or any other sauce you love.

MUSHROOM DRESSING

This is, no holds barred, my favorite dressing. (I'd rather call it stuffing, but I know that technically that's only right if you bake it inside the bird, so dressing it is!) In addition to wild mushrooms, it includes chestnuts and wild herbs.

YIELD: 10 TO 12 CUPS

1½ cups dried mushrooms

4 ounces diced bacon or pancetta

2 cups chopped onions

2 cups chopped celery

1 stick butter

10 ounces peeled, quartered chestnuts

½ cup chopped parsley

1 teaspoon dried bee balm

1 tablespoon dried and rehydrated mugwort (see page 21)

2 teaspoons salt

1 teaspoon ground pepper

1 pound sourdough bread

2 cups stock (chicken, mushroom, vegetable, meat)

Rehydrate the mushrooms by soaking them in hot water for as long as it takes for them to be pliable. Strain off the solids and set the liquid aside. You can use it as part of the broth called for later in the recipe.

Fry the bacon or pancetta and let it drain on a paper towel.

Return the bacon to the pan and add the mushrooms, onions, and celery, then cook over medium heat until soft, adding butter as needed. You may use up to a stick of butter. (This is not a low-fat recipe!)

Remove the mushrooms and vegetables from the heat, then add the chestnuts, parsley, bee balm, mugwort, salt, and pepper. Combine well.

Cut the sourdough bread into 1-inch cubes and add it to the other ingredients. Add the stock to the bread mix, ½ cup at a time, stirring to combine after each addition. Stop when the mixture holds together lightly. You'll probably need 1–1½ cups total.

Spoon the stuffing into a well-greased casserole dish and dot the top with butter. Bake at 375°F for 35–45 minutes or until the top is browned. I know dressing is traditionally served with a holiday turkey, but this is so good, I suggest giving it more time at your table.

MUSHROOM
AND ASPARAGUS BREAD PUDDING

I appreciate recipes that let you use up odds and ends from the refrigerator, and this is one of those recipes. You can use pretty much any mushroom or wild green—and while you're at it, why not play around with your herbs and spices? I love morels and asparagus with sweet clover, porcini and sochan with bee balm, and chanterelles and dock with spicebush berries.

YIELD: 2 (5 X 9-INCH) LOAVES

1 (12–15-ounce) slightly stale loaf Italian or French bread

3 cups milk

2 tablespoons roughly chopped field garlic

3 tablespoons butter, divided

2 cups roughly chopped wild mushrooms

2 cups greens, chopped

4 eggs

1 tablespoon dried sweet clover (or herb of choice)

1 teaspoon salt

½ teaspoon pepper

2 cups crumbled cheese (goat, sharp cheddar, and Parmesan all work well), divided

Preheat the oven to 350°F. Butter the pans and set them aside.

It's important to use stale bread in this recipe or the end result will be mushy. If you don't have stale bread, cut or tear a loaf into rough chunks and leave them out on the counter overnight. Alternatively, toast them lightly. When you're ready to cook, cut the stale bread into smaller pieces (about an inch in diameter) and put them in a large mixing bowl. Set the bowl aside.

Combine the milk and garlic in a saucepan and heat until it just begins to simmer. Remove the pan from the heat, cover, and let it sit for 30 minutes.

While the milk infuses, melt 1 tablespoon of the butter and sauté the mushrooms until they give up all their liquid. Turn off the heat and set the mushrooms aside. If you already have cooked mushrooms left over, you can skip this step, or, if you're using dried mushrooms, rehydrate them and drain from the liquid before cooking.

Barely blanch the greens in boiling water, just until they turn bright green, then dunk them in cold water to stop the cooking.

Strain the milk off the garlic and throw the garlic away. Pour the milk over the bread chunks, stirring to cover all the bread. It will absorb the milk quickly.

Beat the eggs, then add the sweet clover, salt, and pepper. Add this to the bread, along with the greens, mushrooms, and 1½ cups of cheese. Stir to combine all the ingredients, then transfer the mixture into the buttered baking pans. Dot with remaining butter and sprinkle with the remaining cheese.

Bake until the bread is golden brown and puffy; this should take about 50 minutes. Serve the bread pudding warm as a main course or side dish. I often make extra and freeze a loaf for when I don't feel like cooking.

MUSHROOM SAUCE

Mushroom sauces can be chunky or smooth, creamy or wine-based. Start with this recipe, then tweak it any way you like to go with anything you like: pasta, rice, chicken, beef, pork, fish, or stewed vegetables.

YIELD: 3 CUPS

3 tablespoons olive oil

2 cups chopped mushrooms

1 large onion, diced

1 tablespoon minced field garlic

3 tablespoons butter

3 tablespoons flour

1 cup chicken broth (with an extra ½ cup in reserve)

1 tablespoon lemon juice

2 tablespoons mushroom powder

2 teaspoons salt

½ teaspoon pepper

1 cup half-and-half

Add the olive oil to a sauté pan and sauté the mushrooms and onion over medium heat until both are soft. Add the garlic and cook 2 more minutes. Set aside.

In another pan, melt the butter over medium heat and whisk in the flour until you have a golden roux. Add the broth, lemon juice, mushroom powder, salt, and pepper, and whisk until smooth. Add the half and half and bring to a simmer.

For a chunky sauce, combine the mushrooms with the cream-based sauce now. For a smooth sauce, transfer the mushrooms to a blender and process until smooth, then combine with the cream. For this smooth sauce, you'll probably need to add ¼–½ cup more broth to reach the right thickness.

MUSHROOM
VOL AU VENTS

If you need to make a fancy-looking appetizer that is surprisingly easy to put together, try this mushroom puff pastry. *Vol au vents* means "fly on the winds," and it is meant to describe how light and flaky these pastries are. You already know I don't make my own puff pastry, but I *do* always keep a box in the freezer. There are several good, ready-made, frozen puff pastry brands, and using one of them makes this dish a snap.

If you dried your mushrooms to preserve them, rehydrate them in warm water until the texture is tender, and save the liquid to add to future soups or stocks. The amount of time this takes will depend on the size and meatiness of the mushroom.

YIELD: 8 *VOL AU VENTS*

1 sheet puff pastry

2 tablespoons olive oil

1/4 cup slivered onion

1 cup sliced wild mushrooms, fresh or rehydrated

1/2 tablespoon butter

2 tablespoons white wine

1/2 teaspoon salt

1/4 teaspoon pepper

1/4 cup sour cream

1/4 cup cheese of choice (grated if it's hard like Gruyère and crumbled if it's soft like feta)

1 tablespoon plus 1 tablespoon chopped chives

1 egg, beaten

Preheat the oven to 400°F.

Puff pastry is sold frozen, and the working temperature of the dough is important. Thaw puff pastry on a floured cutting board or countertop for 30–40 minutes. More time than that will make it too warm to work with.

While the pastry is thawing, heat the olive oil in a frying pan and sauté the onion until tender and translucent. Add the mushrooms and cook over medium-high heat until they start to brown; you want a little caramelization on the mushrooms. When the mushrooms begin to look golden brown, add the butter. When that has melted, add the wine, salt, and pepper, stirring until the liquid is absorbed. Remove the

continued

mushrooms from the heat. Allow to cool slightly, then fold in the sour cream, cheese, and chopped chives.

Return to the puff pastry. It should be stiff and barely flexible; you don't want a soft and squishy dough. When it has thawed enough to be unfolded, unfold it and roll it out gently with a rolling pin. The resulting rectangle should be about 8 x 12 inches.

Use a glass or biscuit cutter to cut the dough into 16 (2-inch) circles. You could make larger pastries, but I like to keep these bite-sized. Take half of the circles and, using a glass with a 1-inch diameter, cut a smaller circle in the middle of 8 of the circles. Remove the centers, separating them from the rings.

Arrange the larger circles on a parchment paper–covered baking sheet, leaving an inch or two between each circle. Brush each one with the beaten egg, then gently press one of the rings on top of each circle. Prick the bottom of each circle with a fork to prevent it from rising too much in the oven. Arrange the smaller circles (leftover from creating the rings) on the parchment paper and brush them with the egg wash. Bake for 20–25 minutes, or until the pastry is puffy and golden brown.

When the puff pastry cups are cool enough to handle, fill each one with a few tablespoons of the mushroom mixture and top with a smaller circle. Serve warm, to applause and appreciation.

NOTE: Both the puff pastry shells and the mushroom filling can be made a day or two in advance, but not combined. Allow the pastry shells to cool completely, then move the shells and the mushroom filling to separate airtight containers and store in the fridge. Reheat the shells for 5 minutes in a 400°F oven before adding the warmed mushroom filling.

MINI MUSHROOM
POPOVERS

This is a very flexible recipe: use any kind of mushroom with any kind of green. Chickweed and lamb's quarters are mild enough to let the mushroom flavor take center stage, but more strongly flavored greens, like orache and garlic mustard are also delicious. The important thing is that the both greens and mushrooms are chopped very fine.

YIELD: 30 MINI PUFFS

1 cup finely chopped mushrooms

1³⁄₄ cups stock (both chicken and mushroom work well)

¹⁄₂ stick butter

1 teaspoon salt, divided

¹⁄₄ teaspoon ground pepper

³⁄₄ cup flour

1¹⁄₄ teaspoons baking powder

4 eggs

2 tablespoons finely chopped greens

Preheat the oven to 400°F.

In a saucepan, combine the mushrooms and stock and bring the liquid to a boil. Add the butter, ½ teaspoon of salt, and the pepper, then reduce the heat and simmer for 5 minutes, uncovered.

Remove the mushrooms from the heat and whisk in the flour, baking powder, and remaining salt. Mix together well. The batter will be quite stiff. Set the mushroom mixture aside to cool slightly before adding the eggs. (Adding eggs to any hot liquid can cook them, causing the eggs to solidify in small lumps.)

While the mushrooms are cooling, lightly whisk the eggs, then add them gradually to the cooled mushrooms, beating well to make a smooth batter. Next, fold in the greens.

Grease a minimuffin tin and put it in the preheated oven to heat the oil for 5 minutes or until the oil just begins to smoke. It's important that the muffin tin be smokin' hot.

Spoon the batter into each muffin cup, leaving ¼ inch of space at the top. Bake for 15 minutes or until the batter puffs up nicely.

Mushroom puffs make perfect, bite-sized appetizers or a delicious side dish. They even make a great breakfast when served warm with a little butter.

OYSTER MUSHROOM
STEAKS

This recipe is so simple it's barely a recipe. Oyster mushrooms often have very large caps, and it isn't a stretch to think of those caps as steaks. By searing them between two very hot pieces of metal, you caramelize the outside of the steaks while rendering the interior soft, warm, and almost melty.

YIELD: 2 TO 4 SERVINGS

4 large oyster mushroom caps

1 tablespoon olive oil

$1/2$ teaspoon salt

$1/4$ teaspoon pepper

$1/2$ teaspoon ground, dried field garlic

$1/2$ teaspoon dried bee balm

Trim any remnants of stem from the underside of the caps; these mushrooms need to lie flat.

In a bowl, combine the olive oil, salt, pepper, garlic powder, and bee balm and whisk to combine. Place the mushroom caps in the olive oil and allow them to marinate while you prepare the implements.

Heat a cast iron griddle until it is *very* hot. A few drops of water flicked on the griddle should jump around wildly. On a second burner, heat a large, empty cast iron pan over medium-high heat. Place the mushroom caps on the griddle, arranged in such a way that the bottom of the cast iron pan can cover them all. Then put the hot cast iron pan on top of the mushrooms. The weight of the pan will press the mushrooms flat. After 3 minutes, lift the pan to check on the progress. The steaks should be slightly browned and crispy. It may take up to 5–6 minutes.

DEVILED EGGS
WITH BLACK TRUMPETS

You could make this with any strongly flavored mushroom, but the dark color of the black trumpets really stands out against the egg yolks. This dish is perfect for a fancy picnic or any summer lunch.

YIELD: 12 DEVILED EGGS

6 large eggs

2 tablespoons mayonnaise

2 tablespoons sour cream

1 teaspoon Dijon mustard

2 tablespoons olive oil

1 tablespoon finely diced onion or shallot

$1/2$ cup finely chopped black trumpet mushrooms

$1/4$ teaspoon salt

Place the eggs in a pot of cold water and bring to a boil over high heat. (Starting the eggs in cold water prevents them from cracking as they boil.) When the water begins to boil, reduce the heat to medium and set a timer for 10 minutes. Drain the boiled eggs and place them in a bowl of ice water to chill them quickly. Hard-boiled eggs can be refrigerated for up to a week.

When you're ready to assemble the deviled eggs, peel the eggs, slice them in half, and remove the yolks. Set the whites aside.

In a bowl, mash the yolks with a fork, then combine with the mayonnaise, sour cream, and mustard to form a smooth paste. It will be easier to make a smooth yolk filling if you mash the yolks alone first. (Maybe you'll use your own foraged mayo and mustard . . .) Set aside.

Warm the olive oil and cook the onion or shallot over medium-low heat until translucent. Add the mushrooms and cook until tender. Remove from heat and allow them to cool.

Use a spoon or pastry bag to fill the egg white halves with the yolk mixture, then sprinkle the black trumpets on top of the yolks. Serve at room temperature.

NOTE: If you boil the eggs a few days before making this dish, you'll find they're easier to peel without taking chunks out of the egg whites. If you have chickens, your eggs will probably be fresh enough to peel easily without the chill time.

FURTHER READING

. . . .

Backyard Foraging, by Ellen Zachos
The Wildcrafted Cocktail, by Ellen Zachos
The Forager's Harvest, by Samuel Thayer
Nature's Garden, by Samuel Thayer
Incredible Wild Edibles, by Samuel Thayer
Edible Wild Plants, by John Kallas
The Skillful Forager, by Leda Meredith
The Forager's Feast, by Leda Meredith
Regional Foraging Guides from Timber series, various authors
The Idiot's Guide to Foraging, by Mark "Merriwether" Vorderbruggen
The Complete Mushroom Hunter, Gary Lincoff
The Joy of Foraging, Gary Lincoff
Edible Wild Plants of the Prairie, by Kelly Kindscher
Foraging the Mountain West, by Thomas J. Elpel and Kris Reed
Around the World in 80 Plants, by Stephen Barstow
100 Edible Mushrooms, by Michael Kuo
The Neighborhood Forager, by Robert Henderson
Stalking the Wild Asparagus, by Euell Gibbons
The Encyclopedia of Edible Plants of North America, by Francis Couplan
Feasting Free on Wild Edibles, by Bradford Angier
The Edible Wild, by Berndt Berlund and Clare E. Bolsby

Websites

The Backyard Forager (www.backyardforager.com)
Wild Food Girl (www.wildfoodgirl.com)
Leda Meredith (www.ledameredith.com)
Hunger and Thirst (www.hungerandthirstforlife.blogspot.com)
Learn Your Land (www.learnyourland.com)
Foraging Texas (www.foragingtexas.com)
Eat the Weeds (www.eattheweeds.com)
The 3 Foragers (www.the3foragers.blogspot.com)
Edible Leeds (www.edible-leeds.blogspot.com)
Galloway Wild Foods (www.gallowaywildfoods.com)

Miscellaneous

Forager's Harvest (www.foragersharvest.com)
This website (and brick and mortar store) is a forager's dream, selling books, tools, and preserved wild edibles.

The Backyard Forager (www.backyard-forager.thinkific.com)
If you're interested in online foraging courses, I offer several here.

INDEX

· · · · · · · · · · · · · · · ·

METRIC CONVERSION CHART

VOLUME MEASUREMENTS		WEIGHT MEASUREMENTS		TEMPERATURE CONVERSION	
U.S.	METRIC	U.S.	METRIC	FAHRENHEIT	CELSIUS
1 teaspoon	5 ml	½ ounce	15 g	250	120
1 tablespoon	15 ml	1 ounce	30 g	300	150
¼ cup	60 ml	3 ounces	90 g	325	160
⅓ cup	75 ml	4 ounces	115 g	350	180
½ cup	125 ml	8 ounces	225 g	375	190
⅔ cup	150 ml	12 ounces	350 g	400	200
¾ cup	175 ml	1 pound	450 g	425	220
1 cup	250 ml	2¼ pounds	1 kg	450	230